HERMENEUTICAL WOMEN OF MAHASWETA DEVI AND AMBAI

DR. JOHN SUGANYA M | ANITH PREM MALARAVAN. M

Copyright © Dr. John Suganya M, Anith Prem Malaravan. M
All Rights Reserved.

To

The Almighty

Contents

Preface

The study of Mahasweta Devi and Ambai has kindled the interest in Myth, especially to pen this book. The manuscript has focused more on the similarities and dissimilarities amongst the world renowned writers. The very age in which these two writers lived had been categorized as golden age. The eminence character of women is predominantly owing to their works which are appropriate not only for a particular age but also for all ages.

The book has an insight on Mahasweta Devi and Ambai's reshaped women. The selected stories were in detail analyzed with respect to feminine-world of the great writers. Their works have been translated into many languages and believe their comparative study is a worthy exercise.

The Indian English has a long history of resistance and activism in it, which has been carefully crafted in this work of art. It has provided a platform for prospective readers and audience to interact and experience socio-cultural issues along with political tribulations. It has voiced feminist issues with an unbiased and imperial fervor.

Acknowledgements

I would like to acknowledge and thank Dr. Jeyantha Sri Balakrishnan for her advice & guidance to make this work possible.

I would also like to give special thanks to my caring, loving and supportive husband Mr. M. Anith Prem Malaravan & my daughter A.J. Alice Jessie Prejo for their continuous support and understanding to complete this book. Also, I offer appreciation to my scholars Harish Sachin.V, Jeevitha.S, Priyangha.B for their timely help to complete the book.

Finally, I would like to thank God The Almighty, for taking me through all the hitches and let me to publish the book.

Dr. M. John Suganya

I

PROLEGOMENON

Literature is the foundation of life. It places an emphasis on many topics from human tragedies to tales of the ever-popular search for love. While it is physically written in words, these words come alive in the imagination of the mind, and its ability to comprehend the complexity or simplicity of the text. Literature enables people to see through the lenses of others, and sometimes even inanimate objects; therefore, it becomes a looking glass into the world as others view it. It is a journey that is inscribed in pages, and powered by the imagination of the reader. Ultimately, literature has provided a gateway to teach the reader about life experiences from even the saddest stories to the most joyful ones that will touch their hearts.

Literature, as an alternative, is the closest thing the world being able to understand another person whole-heartedly. For instance, a novel about a treacherous war, written in the perspective of a soldier, allows the reader to envision their memories, their pain, and their emotions without actually being the soldier ourselves. Consequently, literature can act as a time machine, enabling individuals to go into a specific time period of the story, into the psyche and soul of the protagonist.

With the ability to see the world with a pair of fresh eyes, it triggers the reader to reflect upon their own lives. Reading a material that is relatable to the reader may teach them morals and encourage them to practice good judgment. An example would be William Shakespeare's stories, where each one is meant to be reflective of human nature – both the good and bad. Consequently, this can promote better judgment of situations, so the reader does not find themselves in the same circumstances as perhaps those in the fiction world. Henceforth, literature is proven to not only be reflective of life, but it can also be used as a guide for the reader to follow and practice good judgment from.

The world today is ever-changing. Never before has life been so chaotic and challenging for all. Life before literature was practical and predictable, but in present day, literature has expanded into countless libraries and into the minds of many as the gateway for comprehension and curiosity of the human mind and the world around them. Literature is of great importance and is studied upon as it provides the ability to connect human relationships, and define what is right and what's wrong. Therefore, words are alive more than ever before.

The first fine translations into English were made in the 14th century by Geoffrey Chaucer, who adapted from the Italian of Giovanni Boccaccio in his own *Knight's Tale* and *Troilus and Criseyde*; began a translation of the French-language *Roman de la Rose*; and completed a translation of Boethius from the Latin. Chaucer founded an English poetic tradition on *adaptations* and translations from those earlier-established literary languages.

The first great English translation was the *Wycliffe Bible* (ca. 1382), which showed the weaknesses of an underdeveloped English prose. Only at the end of the 15th century did the great age of English prose translation begin with Thomas Malory's *Le Morte Darthur*—an adaptation of Arthurian romances so free that it can, in fact, hardly be called a true translation.

The spread of the English language in India has led it to become adapted to suit the local dialects. Due to the large diversity in Indian languages and cultures, there can be instances where the same English word can mean different things to different people in different parts of India. There are three different stages of English Language in India i.e.cultivated, closely approximating: Received Pronunciation and associated with younger generation of urban and sub-urban regions of metropolitan cities of the country;Standard, a social indicator of the higher education, and Regional, associated with the general population, and closely approximating the second-language Vernacular-English variety. The number of languages increased through diversion, and people started to look for ways to communicate, hence the birth of translation is required.

Contemporary literary study has proven way to research on translation and it has started to take another trail, which is more perfunctory. The invention of the Internet, together with the new technological development in communication and digital materials, has increased cultural exchanges between nations. This led translators to look for ways to cope with these changes and to utilize practical techniques that enable them to translate more and waste-less. They also felt the need to enter the world of cinematographic translation, hence have got the birth of audiovisual translation. The latter technique, also called screen translation, is concerned with the translation of all kinds of TV programs, including films, series, and documentaries. This field is based on computers and translation software programs, and it is composed of two methods: dubbing and subtitling. In fact, audiovisual translation marks a turning point in the field of translation.

In short, translation has a very rich history in the West. Since its birth, translation was the subject of much controversy among theorists. Each theorist approaches it from his own ideology and field of study, the fact which gives its history a changing quality.

The translator has the capacity to enhance our understanding of development issues and indigenous cultures by mediating ideas across cultural and national boundaries. Translation is not merely an interlinguistic process. It is more complex than replacing source language text with target language text and includes cultural and educational nuances that can shape the options and attitudes of recipients. Translations are never produced in a cultural or political vacuum and cannot be isolated from the context in which the texts are embedded. As David Katan in *Translating Cultures* comments it: '. . . the translator is a bilingual mediating agent between monolingual communication participants in two different language communities'. Therefore translators not only have to be intermediaries between different language systems, but also have to be intercultural mediators – or as it has been stated by Aniela Korzeniowska and Piotr Kuhiwczak in *Successful Polish-English Translation Tricks of the Trade* – they have to be both 'bilingual and bicultural'. Thus, translation performs a crucial role in understanding the culture.

The role of the translator in mediating source ideas across cultural and national boundaries places him or her in a unique position in particular for understanding a range of development issues. Translating narratives from the global South is an invaluable source of knowledge about unfamiliar languages, indigenous cultures and experiences, and is immensely useful for gaining an understanding of non-European societies. Moreover, translation can also have a critical influence in politics and can act as an agent for reconciliation or social integration.

Quintessential to the translation and its contribution have received the extensive term 'comparative literature', it is gaining much importance in our country, India. It was Prof. Buddhadeva Bose, the noted Bengali writer, who first instigated comparative literature at the Jadavpur University, Calcutta amidst intellectual sceptism. It was practically an unknown subject in India, though it could bring together the regional literatures of our country and shed parochialism. The Fulbright/Smith programmes operated by the government of United States through the U.S. Educational Foundation in India (USEFI) developed this branch of study in India. Comparative Literature, has now taken its roots in Madurai Kamaraj University, where it is recognized as an academic discipline by both the faculties of English and Tamil. Feminism and Humanism are two imperative branches of literary study that fathom the relationship between literature and humans which make the readers see men and women as makers of textual meaning, both in writing and reading. Humanistic psychologists and feminists see the lives of people with an optimistic perspective and focus on the ability of human beings to think consciously and rationally to achieve their full potential.

The feminist movement "includes any form of opposition to any form of social, personal or economic discrimination which women suffer because of their sex" says David Bouchier in the "Introduction" to his book *The Feminist Challenge*. The desire for equality with men on the social and political fronts took the form of an organized movement in the west. It included both the struggle for women's equal rights as well as the aspirations and strivings towards the all-round liberation of women, which is considered emancipation.

In the words of Gerda Lerner in her book *The Creation of Patriarchy*, "feminism is not always a movement, for it can be a level of consciousness, a stance, an attitude, as well as the basis for organized effort". The feminist consciousness is a perception of victimization by the dominating males of the society which leads to women's subordinate status and their consequent oppression. Before India attained independence, conventional Indian women who were not really concerned about their oppression and equal rights did not feel the need for an organised fight for women's rights of equality with men which has continued for almost two decades in the west was not required in India. This was because by the time Indian women had become really conscious of woman's rights, they had been guaranteed social, legal and political rights after independence. Thus it is the second stage, or the all-round liberation, or emancipation of women, that becomes the prime concern of the feminists in India. Generally it is accepted that The Indian Feminists are more humanists than the feminists of the west.

Though the liberation of women is a concept that gathered force in the later-half of the twentieth century, India has a much earlier history and tradition of intellectually emancipated women during the 'Vedic Age'. There were Vedic women like Ghosha, Vach, Lopamudra, Maitreye and others, who were free to pursue scholarly studies and they were called 'Brahmavadinis', who, besides their intellectual and spiritual pursuits, involved themselves actively in the administration, finance, agriculture and crafts of their age. A girl child was welcomed into the midst of her people, and could undergo the same ritualistic observances as men, had the freedom of choice of either marrying or staying single, could choose her sexual partner and was treated with equality and respect with men. This glorious Vedic tradition of equality of those women with their men was lost later.

When the nomadic Aryans became permanent settlers, women were relegated to do household chores, and were kept out of religious and ritualistic performances. Their education and intellectual development were never insisted upon. Perhaps due to their physical frailty and biological functions of procreation that involved them more, women ceased to take up more masculine jobs. The moment women took up mannish jobs, her status decreased, they were considered inferior to men. With the codification of laws by Manu, the subordination of women was assured for centuries to come. Manu's idea that a woman does not deserve freedom, and she has to be protected in her childhood by her father, in her youth by her husband and in her old age by her sons place the seal of male domination and tyranny over women as well as their socially sanctioned oppression.

Thus the present concept of women's liberation is not a novel one to an Indian who is familiar with ancient Indian history and lineage. The efforts to achieve woman's emancipation can be seen as the effort of Indian women to win back their past glorious Vedic tradition of equality with men. Kamala Devi Chattopadhyay opines, in her article *The Status of Women in India* in the book *Women in Modern India.* This movement cannot in any sense be said to be a rebellion or a revolt against man; it is rather than an attempt to regain lost ground. It is not actuated by any spirit of competition nor marked by violence; it is a movement of calm assertion.

The name feminism conjures up an extremely radical, rebellious, anti-male attitude in women. But it need not necessarily be so. Though in western countries feminists emphasize a separatist culture that avoids the influence of men, in India, feminist position does not include any negation of man, or the influence of men in the progressive strides taken by women.

This fact becomes clear when the role of women during the Indian freedom struggle is observed. English education was popularized during the British rule helped in making Indian men reflect on the oppressive conditions of their women in society. Men like Raja Ram Mohan Roy, who struggled for the abolition of Sati, Iswar Chandra Vidya Sagar, Keshav Chandra Sen, and a host of others clamoured for reforms to put an end to the practice of child marriage, ill treatment of widows and ban on widow re-marriage, and also M.K.Gandhi, the leader of the National Freedom Movement, was a great supporter of women's liberation. These men, while trying to remove such evil practices, were also involved in educating and raising the status of Indian women. In *Women and Social Injustice* he says: These questions of liberation of women, liberation of India, removal of untouchability, amelioration of economic condition of the masses and the like resolve themselves into penetration into the villages and reconstruction or rather reformation of village life.

Gandhiji, formerly known as M.K.Gandhi was concerned about liberation at the grass roots level. But he also gave an impetus to his ideal of 'stree-shakti' when he called upon all Indian women to come out of the confines of their homes and contribute their mite to the freedom struggle. This was taken as a challenge by many women to break their century's old, confined existence. Among the Indian middle class women who were educated, this led to an awakening of their inner selves, and the consequent arousal of a feminist consciousness. Feminism or the concept of the liberation for women from their traditional restrains in society has yet to percolate down to the lower strata of Indian women who are not sufficiently educated. For many Indian women, it is a question of stark survival. And yet, due to the efforts of the social reformists and the gaining popularity of higher education and the resultant economic independence among girls, the concept of equality and liberation is slowly gaining ground in the Indian soil.

A feminist perspective requires having a brief overview of the major western feminist trends that have influenced the women of the East also, especially Indian women. Western critics have mainly delineated seven varieties of feminist thought: Liberal, Marxist, Socialist, Radical, Psycho analytical, Existential and Post-modern Feminism. There are also other categories of western feminisms like individual feminism, relative feminism, cultural feminism, and lesbian separatism.

The concept of feminism or women's liberation is never static. What was once considered a part of a radical stand in feminism may in course of time become a moderate view. So, the type of feminism adopted by a particular group of people depends a lot on their socio-cultural and regional background, and the particular type of oppression that they have to face due their culture and tradition as well as their geographical locality. Thus, the democratic liberal feminists of England and America, like Mary Wollstonecraft and Margaret Fuller, the Marxist feminist of Russia like Alexandra Kollontai and American socialist feminists Charlottle Perkins Gilman and Zilla Eisenstein, also have the French feminists like Simone De Beauvoir, Helene Cixous and Nancy Chodorow. There is a black feminist ideology which they prefer to call 'womanism' that deals with the specific problems of black African women. There is also the Scandinavian variety of feminism that gives more importance to the 'difference' between man and woman rather than the similarity emphasized by feminists who follow the androgynous paradigm like Virginia Woolf. Going by these facts, could possibly isolate a typical Indian variety of feminism that is an offshoot of the Indian cultural ethos and its past traditions.

Modern feminist trends in the west have moved beyond the petty politics of equal rights and opportunities. The study on 'feminism' or women's liberation is a term that escapes clear definition, last it depends on the individual, one's culture, the place one belongs to, and how far one is able to practice one's feminist ideals. Indian feminism seems to follow a middle path that stands between the extreme radical feminist stance and the liberal, individual, socialist and cultural feminist stances.

On the other hand the suffering of the tribals involved the individual suffering for the community of the tribal group and the community suffering for the individual. They are seen celebrating their inheritance in their own style. They have their individual aesthetics in pastoral and simple forms. They have developed their personal aesthetics. *The adivasis*, the tribals of India or aborigines, have a very rich tradition of dance, music and folklore in particular. By way of new elucidations, they could restructure their image and identity of this tradition. They are making an effort to build their own aesthetics which reflects their insights of life and world around them.

Although the caste system has been abolished under the Indian constitution, even now there is inequity and injustice against tribals. Major steps have been taken to provide opportunities in jobs and education since Indian Independence. To improve the conditions of tribals many social organizations have promoted practical requirements through improved education, health and employment. Despite the fact that various development measures have been taken to improve the status of tribals, the transformation has not changed the Indian convention.

Men and women are the vital parts of God's creation. They are the two sides of a coin. It is believed down the ages by the society that one without another is merely like a body without spirit, a ship without a rudder or a flower without a fragrance. Woman is no longer considered a toy in man's hands. She is creating her individuality in all facets of life. Indian women novelists have given a new dimension to Indian literature. In addition to making a mark in many fields, women have also proclaimed a new awareness in the field of literature. In general they have contributed vastly to Indian Writing in English predominantly in fiction and their contributions are impressive.

Surendra Narayan Jha remarks in the article "The Treatment of Modern Women in Indian Novel and Manju Kapur's *Difficult Daughters*": "since time immemorial man-woman relationship has been a cherished goal for the creative writers all over the world." He also quotes Aristotle's views on women: "the female is female by virtue of certain deficiency" and Saint Thomas Aquinas' remarks on woman in multilevel angles and Dale Splender states in his book *Man Made Language* that "women has been fundamentally oppressed by male-dominated language".

S.Prasanna Sree quotes Jawaharlal Nehru's words in her article "An Introduction to Women and Women Writing in English: we talk of revolution- political and economic and yet the greatest revolution in a country is one that effects improvement in the status and living conditions of its women".

Women comprise half of the world's population. They are ironically not treated equally with men in all fields of human activity, even though women work hard to develop family, husband and children, they are marginalized, suppressed and oppressed to avail the opportunities for satisfying their lives. This distressing picture of woman is not distinctive only to India but it is the same difficult position women through the world find themselves in.

In her article "The Feminist Perspective: The Indian Situation and its Literary Manifestations," Jasbir Jain comments on men's role in patriarchal society: Men in patriarchal societies have deprived of a whole range of experience, of having to reach out to the other. They have looked only at themselves having reduced women to subordinate positions. Men— both socially and intellectually—can be a powerful medium of change. For instance, R.K. Narayan's novels, to give an example, reveal on ever-growing awareness of the need to expand the area of a woman's freedom.

Woman was believed to be an ultimate wife, a mother and an outstanding home-maker with different roles in the family, in a male-dominated society. Sacrifice, service, obedience and tolerance are essential qualities that are expected from her as wife and mother. She evinces too much of patience and modifies her life faithfully and submissively which is appreciated in general by anybody in the society. Her personal nature has very little acknowledgement in the patriarchal society and so behaving in a humble manner is her natural way of life.

In "Reading Resistance," Shoba venkatesh Ghosh avers, "Women participate, too, in various oppressions. And with the sensibility that characterizes the paradigm of gender (because of its entanglements with caste, class or religion), it is quite conceivable that a woman may in varying situations move between positions of powerlessness and power".

On the other hand women were encouraged to emulate the epic archetypes of Sita and Draupadi, who were symbolic of absolute fidelity. There was an anxiety to preserve the image of woman as the epitome of all that was pure and chaste. Most of the Indian women stuck to the traditional values even if they were highly educated and were exposed to modern ideas also tried to assimilate modern ideas without casting away their traditional values.

Inspite of all these changes, the condition of the tribal women has not yet changed. Tribal women are oppressed on several levels. Although in most tribal societies in India, position of women is relatively better than in Hindu caste society, property is still transmitted through the male line, and in general, women do not have access to political power. Moreover, the sanscritization process, where by lower castes adopt some of the customs and practices of the upper-caste such as dowry, purdah, restrictions on remarriage and on relations between men and women, has severely eroded the tribal women's social and economic status.

Women are also oppressed because they belong to a group considered inferior because of its ethnic or caste position. In the Santhal Parganas, tribals are considered sub-human creatures by the non-tribals. Their land can be usurped, their possessions can be looted and they can with impunity be laughed at and pushed aside. The oppressed women are used by those who have the power to subjugate their people by rape, torture and forced prostitution. The landowners employ police to humiliate, punish, and establish control over an entire community which is economically and materially dependent. The rape and sexual exploitation of adivasis women by Hindus and Muslims are a violation and humiliation for the entire social group. The rape of adivasis women by non-adivasis men can also be seen as an attempt to control female sexuality. Statistically, women do not comprise a minority or marginal cluster. Women do not have the benefit of equivalent position and individual self-respect in the male-dominated world either in India or in other countries, which makes them insignificant- socially, politically, sexually and culturally. Ultimately their sexual abuse leads to social, political and economic abuse. Women who fit into the weaker sectors of society cope with twofold exploitation, double inequality and twin injustice thus theirs is a dual risk. Gender being the source of their marginality, they face dehumanization and humiliation, confront household aggression too.

In family life, husbands and wives are uneven partners, the relation or relationship that exists among mother, father; sister, brother; son, daughter; husband, wife and in-laws is one of the finest creations of man. The relationship gives certain protection to women, else they would have been the sufferers of male desire, but the women suffer so much under the dark phallic shade of desire of man. All these problems are dealt with in feminism. Empowerment of Women is talked by everyone, can be attained only through equality, employment and education.

The apprehension of women writers is bare body and naked soul of woman. In order to oppress the women, the male-dominated world has used religion, culture and social order. In fact, all marginalized and oppressed groups of people face the problems of human rights abuse which finally leads to dehumanisation, if it is not opposed and fought vociferously. Meera Bai in "Women's voices: The Novels of Indian Women Writers" writes about the state of women: Most of the Indian women stick to the traditional values even if they are highly educated and are exposed to modern ideas. They try to assimilate modern ideas without casting away their traditional values.

Bhabani Bhattacharya's novels portray women facing the crisis of value adaptation in the process of transition from the old to the new. Though he seems to be more concerned with the problems that new India is facing in the process of progress, his novels show an awareness of the Indian woman's capacity for adaptability and suffering as well as her power to sublimate. Bhabani Bhattacharya writes, I think the women of India have more depth, more richness than men, the transition from the old to the new, the crisis of value adaptation strikes deeper into the lives of our women than our men folk.

In order to improve the conditions of the downtrodden and deserted sections of the society like women of scheduled castes and scheduled tribes, the freedom struggle produced an impulse in the Indian male and female. Thus, when the constitution for an independent India was illustrated, the importance was put on the development of a democratic society. Maya Majumdar has quoted the articles which are meant for human rights in his book "Social Status of Women in India". Articles 14, 150, 16, 39(e) and 51 were introduced for the abolition of discriminatory and offensive practices against women. These Articles gave assurance to the equality and special protection for women. The universal declaration of Human Rights was implemented on 10th December, 1948 and its Article 1 offered that "all human beings are born free and equal in dignity and rights". Article 2 which meant for equality of sexes states that "everyone is entitled to all the rights and freedom without distinction of sex". Article 3 highlights that "covenant states should agree to make sure equal rights of men and women."

In pre-independence days some women had willingly decided against marriage in order to dedicate their life to the national cause or social service. Today a number of successful unmarried women enjoy high status in the professions, services and in the field of social work. Whereas married women class unite housework and job, take a job after their children have grown up. New standard of living of women is obvious now.

The rate of change in the point of view of women working outside home or participating in public life has been slow and unequal. These approaches are related to perceptions about natural attitudes and abilities of women, her proper field of work, man-woman relationships. When women first entered the films or the professional theatre, the very idea had been scowled by almost all sections of the community. Merely particular castes and communities were allowed to participate in domestic performances in many regions, those women were professional dancers and singers.

Although the discrimination still continues, the situation has improved now. Long ago, dancing and singing were associated only with courtesans, but slowly with the cultural reawakening they have become more acceptable to society. Recently, women have done well in administrative jobs too, but, the difficulties in this field are of different nature. At the maximum, men are prepared to admit a woman as an equal, but still men do not enjoy working under a woman superior.

While writing on fiction of women in India, and compiling anthologies of writings of women, have often looked for commonalities of themes, or complementarities in the negotiation of narrative, language, and form among women writers across the country. Indian feminist writers gained attention of the world literature and attained the phenomenal success. The women writers are looked upon for their daring attempts, frankness to give a glimpse of unexplored psyche of female.

Sylvia Plath, Toni Morrison, Alice walker, Virginia Woolf, Edith Wharton, Katherine Mansfield, Simon de Beauvoir, Kamala Markandeya Nayantra Sahgal, Anita Desai, Shashi Despande, Raja Rao, Rabindranath Tagore, R.K.Narayan, Mulk Raj Anand, Taslima Nasreen, Bapsi Sidwa, Mahasweta Devi, Amrita Pritam, Pratibha Roy, Vaidehi, Indira Gowsami, Ambai, Rajam Krishnan, Chudamani Raghavan, Asoka Mithran have marked brand for feminist writing.

To respect honour and treat everybody with brotherly love is a paramount concern in our society that ironically brands some as untouchables. To uphold humanity to a highest level, Mahasweta Devi and Ambai poured out their longings in their works to awaken the people from the bondage of meaningless old traditions and culture. Their aim and purpose of writing is to uplift the status of the people. In God's eyes everybody is noble and equal. To put a long message of equality to the world audience, the authors have taken extraordinary pains and have given the most important message that is to honour every individual with equal love and affection.

Mahasweta Devi and Ambai are known as conscious writers, because they deal with day-to-day or present issues. They do not struggle to have a separate identity or personality, but they want their female characters and issues to be noticed and recognized. They think globally of local crisis. Their characters are not for lamentation, they stand formally to show that this is their way of treatment for crisis, through their female characters tell the rights of women clearly. It is right of women to bear child, when, to whom and how many. Their characters are known for their alertness, very vigilant ladies, not ready to be sympathized rather they want to war for their rights, for their voice, position in the family and in the society. In the present era more women are educated. They began to write and give expressions and demand education for women. They emphasized the need for change in conditions of woman and philosophy of life.

Their writings kindled positive thinking in the readers. Through the characters the writers have made readers to nod with wisdom and argument. Their characters force the average Indian readers out of their typical Indian complacency regarding gender issues. Because the characters are very firm, strong, stern and more serious. But they are handled with a sense of balance, never disregarding our Indian tradition, yet discovering that there is more in the offering. They try to demystify the mystery. They are voicing not only for the marginalized but for female in middle class too, because there is still poverty, unemployment, illiteracy, discrimination when it comes to women. So their themes and settings are usually the everyday world of a middle class family. Their language is not artificial, but a natural rendition of how it is used in India. Interspersed with local words the language lends authenticity and flavor to write. Few writers are not ready to write beyond their experiences, some are not ready to go near the experiences; some writers go in search of experience and try to evolve of the experience that they have gained. Mahasweta and Ambai belong to the third category, they face the problem, identify the problem, and gives solution to the problem. Like the inner call of wisdom that Jesus, Mother Teresa, Buddha had forced the writers to be experienced. And with the experience they diagnosed the problem to become therapeutic writers.

Mahasweta Devi is one of the greatest literary personalities among the Indian women writers who have given a dimension to the Indian Literature through their works. She voiced the voice of the voiceless. Her works are the conglomeration of various thoughts, opinions, ideas and ideals that are prevailing in the society. And in every work she very clearly and at the same time artistically advocates the philosophy of love and equality. The essence of her work reveals the meaning, spelling and spirit of individual magnanimity. To reveal the false malady of tribals from the society, Mahasweta Devi very carefully and diligently echoed her inner urge. With hope in the axiom that pen is mightier than the sword the author has chosen the path of writing. Her works are very poignant in chiseling a modern brave new world in which every citizen can walk and breathe majestically.

Mahasweta Devi, an Indian social activist and writer was born on January 14, 1926 in Dhaka to literary parents in a Hindu Brahmin family. Her father Manish Ghatak was a well-known poet and novelist. He is the elder brother of the noted film-maker Ritwik Ghatak. Her mother Dharitri Devi was also a writer and a social worker whose brothers were renowned in various fields, such as the noted sculptor Sankha Chaudhury and the founder-editor of the Economic and Political Weekly of India, Sachin Chaudhury. She had her schooling in Dhaka, but after the separation of India she moved to west Bengal in India. She joined the Vishvabharati University which was founded by Rabindranath Tagore in Santiniketan and completed B.A. (Hons) in English, and then finished M.A. in English at Calcutta University. Then, she married the famous playwright Bijon Bhattacharya who was one the founding fathers of the IPTA movement. In the year 1948, she gave birth to Nabarun Bhattacharya, one of Bengal's and India's leading intellectual novelists at present.

In a literary career spanning over 40 years, she has produced 20 collections of short stories and nearly 100 novels in Bengali. Her works have been translated into major Indian languages like Hindi, Urdu, Gujarati, Kannada, Telugu, Malayalam, Marathi and Oriya, and foreign languages like English, Italian, Japanese and French.

Mahasweta Devi was bestowed the Sahitya Akademi Award in 1979 for the novel Aranyer Adhikar. Padma Shri was awarded to her in 1986, the Jnanpith Award, the highest literary award in India from the Bharatiya Jnanpith in 1996, the Ramon Magsaysay Award, considered the Asian equivalent to the Nobel Prize, for Journalism, Literature and the Creative Communication Arts in 1997, Honoris casusa by Indira Gandhi National Open University (IGNOU) in 1999, Padma Vibhushan Award, the second highest civilian Award from the Government of India in 2006, Yashwantrao Chavan National Award in 2010, Bangabibhusan- the highest civilian Award from the Government of west Bengal in 2011 and Hall of Fame Lifetime Achievement Sahityabramha - the first Lifetime Achievement Award in Bengali Literature from 4th screen - IFJW in 2012. Mahasweta Devi has donated the entire prize money from the Jnanpith and Magsaysay awards to the organizations working for the upliftment of the tribal communities.

The Bengali activist, Mahasweta Devi is an exclusive writer among Indian writers. She portrays the tussles of the subalterns, who fight for their basic human rights. She regards women as one amongst the oppressed and in her writings she also deals with women's suppression related to the terms of caste and class. Women bearing the impact of social and political subjugation and who struggle with strong will are portrayed in her works.

Ganesh N Devy avers about the nature of Mahasweta Devi in "The Adivasi Mahasveta" Mahasweta, more a woman of film songs than of ragas, of laughter than long-faced pontificating, is closer to that this reveals than that which decorates and conceals. And yet she is completely detached from everything. You cannot please her by praise or by providing her with creature comforts. She is almost not there when one thinks she is very much there... Mahasweta brought to those poor and harassed people a boundless compassion, to which they instantly understood. Though they could neither speak her language, nor she theirs. She has a Strange ability to communicate with the silenced, her best speech reserved for those to whom no one has spoken.

Today tribals are estimated as eighty million and they are found in several regions of the country. Mahasweta Devi has explored in her novels the history of the trials like Santhals, Hos, Oraons, Kurunis, Mundas and other tribal communities. Mahasweta Devi has been involving herself in the struggles of tribals and also underprivileged communities in the border areas of the states of Bihar, Orissa and West Bengal since 1976.

Sandeep Bhatnagar writes in the review of *Bitter Soil* in "Literature with a Mission" about Mahasweta Devi's concern for the tribal people: Having worked amongst tribals for the greater part of life, she is in a position to articulate the concerns of the dispossessed in the manner of a concerned insider, rather than that of a condescending outsider. She writes in the introduction to *Bitter Soil:* 'I belief in documentation... After reading my work, the reader should face the truth of facts, and feel duly ashamed of the true face of India'.

Mahasweta Devi analyses that the most important reason for the exploitation of the supposed lower classes is the unequal distribution of land. She avers, "The upper caste landowners are still feudal as they were (prior to independence), abiding by values which are against women and the so-called lower castes".

Apart from stories and novels, she has written plays and stories for children as well. In all her writings, she tries to depict the life of tribal men and women. She also writes about Adivasi people like the Sandhals, Lodhas, and Shabars etc. she is extremely dedicated and devoted to these tribes. In her meetings, conferences and writings, she urges the people to stand up for their rights and resist abuse. She demands equality of human rights and encourages these people, especially girls to educate themselves.

Mahasweta Devi started writing stories at a very young age and her writings were published in various literary journals. She has been a regular contributor to *Bortika*, a journal dedicated to the cause of the oppressed and the downtrodden. She selects the plots of her stories from ordinary life around her. The downtrodden the untouchables and the landless tribals who are oppressed and exploited by the upperclass landlords and moneylenders are the heroes and heroines of her stories. In some her stories, she has also dealt with the misrule of the British government and the freedom movement. She also says that the Naxalite Movement of the 1960s and 1970s in Bengal has been a great inspiration for her. Dr. Sharada Iyer quotes in her article "Mahasweta Devi: Mother of 1084 Naxalbari and after".

Mahasweta Devi's interview to Samik Bandopadhyay: Once I became a professional writer, I felt increasingly that a writer should document his own time and history. The socio-economic history of human development has always fascinated me... The Naxalite movement between the late sixties and nearly seventies with its urban phase climaxing in 1970-71, was the first major event after I became a writer that I felt an urge and an obligation to document.

Mahasweta Devi's writings are indeed an expression of her personality and they enable one to form and formulate the autobiography of Mahasweta Devi. In short, her works give expression to her life and reveal her deep dedication for the upliftment of the tribals, downtrodden and untouchables. Mahasweta Devi states in "I am interested in History: I have to sell my writing and thus I could live and eat and provide for others. So I have written plenty of trash. If you count my entire book, I don't think you will find many of them should have been written but I am not ashamed of them either, because I am a professional writer. In Bengal I am the only professional writer who lives by writing and I am proud of that fact."

In the year 1964, Mahasweta Devi began her teaching career at Bijoygarh College, which is an affiliated college of the University of Calcutta. In those days, Bijoygarh College was an institution for working class women students. She also worked as a journalist and as a creative writer during that period. In recent times, she is more famous for her work related to the study of the Lodhas and Shabars, the tribal communities of West Bengal. She is also an activist and she dedicated herself to the struggles of tribal people in Bihar, Madhya Pradesh and Chattisgarh. Mahasweta Devi often depicts the brutal oppression and venal government officials in her elaborate Bengal fiction. Her life in the ordinary people and the inspiration she got from them made her write about the exploited and suffering people.

Mahasweta Devi made a passionate inaugural speech at the Frankfurt Fair in the year 2006, in which she moved the audience to tears with her lines taken from the film song by Raj Kapoor: "This is truly the age where the Joota (shoe) is Japani (Japanese), Patloon (pants) is Englistani (British), the Topi (hat) is Roosi (Russian), But the Dil... Dil (heart) is always Hindustani (Indian... My country, Torn, Tattered, Proud, Beautiful, Hot, Cold, Sandy, Shinning India. My country."

Mahasweta Devi has recently been leading the movement against the industrial policy of the government of West Bengal, the state of her home. In particular, she has harshly criticized the taking away of large tracts of fertile agricultural land from farmers by the government and giving up the land at throwaway prices to industrial houses. She has linked the policy to the commercialization of Santiniketan of Rabindranath Tagore, where she spent her formative years. Because of her, a number of intellectuals, artists, writers and theatre workers joined together in protesting the controversial policy of the government particularly its implementation in Singur and Nandigram. Mahasweta Devi's works for which English translations are available are: *The Queen of Jhansi* (biography, translated in English by Sagaree and Mandira Sengupta from the 1956 first edition in Bangla *Jhansir Rani*), *Hajar Churashir* Ma (*Mother of 1084, 1975*), *Aranyer Adhikar* (The occupation of the forest, 1977), *Agnigarbha* (*Womb of Fire*), *Bitter Soil, Four stories*, Translated by Ipsita Chandra (1998), *Chotti Munda evam Tar Tir (Choti Munda and His Arrow*,1980) Translated by Gayatri Chakravorty Spivak, *Imaginary Maps*, Translated by Gayatri Chakravorty Spivak, (1995), *Dhowli* (short atory), *Dust on the Road*, Translated by Maitreya Ghatak. *Our Non- veg cow* (1998), Translated by Paramita Banerjee, *Bashai Tudu*, Translated by Gayatri Chakravorty Spivak and Samik Bandyopadhyay, 1993), *Titu Mir, Rudali, Breast Stories*, Translated by Gayatri Chakravorty Spivak, 1997, *Of Women, Outcasts, Peasants, and Rebels*, Translated by Kalpana Bardhan, 1990, *Six Stories, Ekkori's Dream*, translated by Lila Majumdar, 1976, *The Book Of The Hunter* (2002), *Outcast* (2002), In Other Worlds: Essays in Cultural Politics, 1987, Translated by Gayatri Chakravorty Spivak, *Till Death Do Us Part, Old Women, Kulaputra*, Translated Into Kannada by Sreemathi H.S., *The Why –Why Girl*, Dakatey Kahini.

Films which are based on Mahasweta Devi's works are *Sunghursh (1968)*, based on her history, which presented a fictionalized account of vendetta within a Thuggee cult in the city of Varanasi, *Rudaali* (1993), *Hazaar Chaurasi Ki Maa* (1998), Maati Maay (2006), based on her story *Daayen, Gangor* (2010) directed by Italo Spinelli, based on her short story, Choli Ke Peeche, from the Book, *Breast Stories.*

Minoli Salgado remarks about Mahasweta Devi in her article "Tribal Stories, Scribal Worlds: Mahasweta Devi and the Unreliable Translator": Mahasweta Devi is probably the most widely translated Indian writer of an indigenous language today. Now recognized as the foremost living writer in Bengali, she has taken up the case of the tribal people of India through political activism and writing. She has spent over thirty years working with and for the tribal people of West Bengal and the southeast of Bihar as a political anthropologist, investigative journalist and editor of a people's magazine.

Beyond the year 1980, Mahasweta Devi has been dynamically linked with many social movements which questions about the bonded labour, leading feudalism in rural society, state negligence and forceful acquirement of agricultural land. She was the vanguard of many movements, particularly those which deal with tribal mobilization, the matter that is near her heart. Her literary works have been recognized with various state and national level credits, and rightfully she was awarded the Padma Vibhushan and the Magsaysay award for her social activism. She believes her writing to be an expansion of her dedication to social work.

The endeavor of the subaltern historians was to focus on the history and tradition of the tribals and other marginalized people. The name of Mahasweta Devi strikes one's mind as one gazes at the hard work of the Indian writers who dedicate themselves to help the indigenous people to revitalize their past and procure them a place of honour in society.

Mahasweta Devi's endeavor is to highlight the customs and history of the tribals of Chotanagpur region, which the mainstream society knows only to some extent, despite the sacrifice and liability of the tribals. For example, the tribals took part in several resistance movements and rebellions against the colonial masters and sacrificed their lives for the country. But, these movements and their leaders were not noticed by the mainstream writers. The endeavor of Mahasweta Devi is to channelize their history into the mainstream society. To acknowledge the importance and prominence of tribal life is the aim of her advocacy.

Anand writes in the article, "Re-visioning History: Mahasweta Devi's *Aranyer Adhikar*" about Mahasweta Devi: As a writer, Mahasweta has a deep sense of history and is a firm believer in documentation and her fiction is based on extensive reading of history. She says, "History fascinates me. Whenever possible I study dates, statistics, government gazettes, human rights laws, laws regarding tribals..." however, her writings on tribal history draw one's attention because they enable one to look at history in a different way.

Mahasweta Devi's observation, her energetic field work, her journalism, her personal life and her creative writing are well balanced. She visits the tribal huts regularly and maintains an open house for the poor and the deprived people. She engages herself keenly in protecting and extending the people's culture embedded in the soil, which is exposed by the violence of a disgraced mainstream society.

Unlikely many Indian writers prefer to observe the chaos of existence from a lofty high distance. But Mahasweta Devi, a former lecturer in English Literature has actively involved herself with human lives. She has worked with Kheria-Shabar tribals in Purulia, West Bengal, for over a quarter of a century and speaks of them with passion.

In Maharashtra, Mahasweta Devi met the Pardhis, Wardars, Bhamtes, Bairagis and Kaikadis. She went to police stations to lodge complaints of rape, torture and humiliation, often against those whose job it was to protect people. She visited sites of old and fresh violence. She brought to those poor and harassed people a boundless compassion, which they instantly understood even though they could neither speak her language nor she theirs.

The pioneering truths of Mahasweta Devi's stories through the classes and traditions portrayed in a mixture of tribal, folk, and urban Bengali lift up her stories from area of rare and evil practicality to that of art-emotion that looks for deliverance as a constant mission. Agony consists of torture and pain. It is a sign of disaster. But experiences of disaster and suffering can irritate the sufferer to rebel and resist. Opposition is an agency of christening and defining the sufferer's identity. The salvation of the sufferer lies in such christening and defining moments. It is high time for activists and the privileged, who rarely see that there is a redemptive price in the pain of the sufferer to learn from the subaltern whose designation, is suffering.

In her exploration for her novel *Jhansir Rani* she recollects the residents who stayed in the area, families who are habitually reliant on the previous upper classes and Bundelkhandi poets who sang of the Queens bravery even now. This contradictory tale moves together with Mahasweta Devi's faith in the prospect of innovative action and she later went on to end other anti- colonial uprisings in novels like *Aranyer Adhikar* and *Titu Mir*. In the first two decades of Mahasweta Devi's writing career, *Aranyer Adhikar* is regarded as a significant milestone.

Mahasweta Devi's disillusionment with middle class happened in her life as her active political dedication that directed her to journey deep into tribal area of Bihar and West Bengal empathize the real situations of tribal life. Throught this period she retired from her more literary activities and her teaching, and in its place produced creative volumes of domineering journalism. This period reached a termination in her starting the essential working- class periodical *Bortika* in which she was in charge of editorial column representing marginal writing that consists of tribals, rural peasants and factory workers. Her acquirements and affection for tribals rapidly increased during the time she lived in areas like Palamu, Murshidabad, Medinipur, and Purulia.

She wishes to stress to these people that the custom of these revolutions is not as important as the need to restore belief in one's own tribal identity. These tribes, who are today an oppressed, disinherited lot, were once fiercely independent, jealously guarding the cultural purity of their race.

With regard to her focus on the tribals and their way of life what Mahasweta Devi ststed at the Frankfurt Book Fair in 1986 is quoted by Anjum Katyal in *The Metamorphosis of Rudali*: As a writer I feel a commitment to my times, to mankind and to myself... for the last fourteen years I have written almost exclusively about the bonded labourers and the tribals, and about repression and protest, about their heroic endeavour for survival and their rights. I must have written a few hundred stories and twenty five novels around these themes... "Noted for her astute perception of the human mind and its complexities, Ambai's writings take readers on a deep unforeseen journey. They startle with their minimalist style in concert with inspired, memorable endings"- Katha prize series. Among the few writers who have emerged to forge Tamil language for different uses and to register fresh thoughts about life and creation during the second half of the twentieth century. C.S.Lakshmi- alias Ambai stands foremost in the arena of Tamil Literature. C.S.Lakshmi was born in 1944 in Coimbatore in a conservative Brahmin family as the third child. She completed her schooling in Bangalore. She inherited her love for Tamil language and culture from her self-taught grandmother and her mother who had the habit of reading popular Tamil journals and her love for Tamil literature from her teacher, Nagammaiyar.

She began writing fiction at the age of sixteen. She participated in a competition organised by the journal 'Kannan'. Her novel *Nanthimalai Saralile* which won the first prize was published in the same journal. The novel was written in "adventure style", under her pen name 'Ambai'. C.S.Lakshmi assumed this pseudonym, following the example of the heroine of Devan's short story, 'Parvathi Sangalpam' which she read at that time in Ananda Vikatan. The woman protagonist, Parvathi of Devan's story was deserted by her husband on account of her 'inferior intelligence', Parvathi, later began writing under the pseudonym Ambai and became famous; when her husband wished to return to her afterwards, she rejected him. The name 'Ambai' is one of the names of Goddess Devi. C.S.Lakshmi admired the determination and independent spirit of Parvathi and decided to assume 'Ambai' as her nom de plume. She was happier for the choice when she became to know that it was also the name of the indomitable Amba of *The Mahabharatha*.

While doing her graduation in Bangalore, she continued to write short stories for Ananda Vikatan. Her second novel *Anthi Malai* which she wrote for 'Kalaimagal Narayaswami Iyar Novel Competitions' won her second prize. Thus two of her novels were published before she was twenty. She did M.A. in Christian College. Her hostel life added to her experience. While working as a school teacher in Banrutti, she became acquainted with a few writers of children's writers' association. But she could not write any story, as she had to engage herself totally in school activities. Her independent spirit and non- conventional outlook incurred the displeasure of the school managing board. She had to resign her job. Then she began an English Tutor in Thiagarayar College in Chennai. After a short period of six months, she joined Delhi University to do Ph.D. on American Studies under UGC fellowship. She resumed writing short stories and dramas, with the encouragement and moral support from her fellow writers. Many of her short stories were published in 'Kanaiyazhi' and 'Kasadathapara'. She taught for a while at a college in Delhi and completed her Doctorate at Jawaharlal Nehru University. Until 1974, she bestowed her performances in classical music and dance.

She devoted herself completely to writing then. She now writes fiction under the pseudonym 'Ambai' and other creative and critical articles under her original name C.S.Lakshmi; she has always distinguished Ambai as writer of fiction and C.S.Lakshmi as cultural anthropologist and critic.

Ambai is acquainted with four languages - Tamil, English, Hindi and Kannada and has travelled widely all over India. She has had long associate with leading Tamil writers of her time such as Indira Parthasarathy, Kasturi Rangan, Vanna Nilavan, Venkat Saminathan, Sudamani and Rajam Krishnan. Her writings have been shaped by her association with these contemporary Tamil writers. At the age of thirty two, she married Vishnu Mathur, a film director while she was working as a lecturer in a college in Delhi. Two years later, she settled in Mumbai and her experiences of writing scripts for her husband's films further shaped her literary mind. She has also read widely and extensively the writings of many Tamil writers and has interviewed many Tamil writers for her research studies. These experiences have developed her critical thinking and enabled her to write stories with different perspectives.

Besides novel, Ambai has published three collections of short stories; *Sirakukal Muriyum (Wings Can Break)* (1976), *Veetin Moolaiyil Oru Samaiyalarai (A Kitchen in the Corner of a House)* (1988), and *Kattil Oru Man (A Deer in the Forest)* (2000) and a critical work in English, *The Face Behind the Mask* (1984). She was a regular contributor to the literary journal 'Kanaiyazhi' and was actively associated with 'Pregnayai' in Chennai.

Ambai disowns her early writings, as their style, language and themes are traditional. "Ambai, a comparative new-comer to the ranks of women writers of short stories, experiments with psychological enquiry into human conditions as they affect the individual and the family". Her experimentation with new language, new themes, and new techniques begins only with *Sirakukal Muriyum*. She is at present recognized as one of the most original writers in Tamil and also as a writer with feminist base.

Ambai, as C.S.Lakshmi, has published many research papers, articles and books on women. She has been an independent researcher in women's studies for more than thirty years. Her work *The Face Behind the Mask: Women in Tamil Literature* (1984) is a study of the images of women in modern Tamil fiction. She has also worked on an illustrated social history of the women of Tamilnadu. She has published An Idiom of Silence: An Oral History and Pictoral Study under a Homi Bhabha Fellowship. In a three-volume oral history series Seven Seas and Seven Mountains containing detailed interviews with fifty notable Indian Women artists, C.S.Lakshmi has authored the first two volumes: The Singer and the Song : Conversations with Women Musicians (2000) and Mirrors and Gestures : Conversations with Women Dancers 92003). She has contributed articles and book reviews to 'The Economic and Political Weekly', 'The Times of India', 'Free Press Bulletin' and 'The Hindu'. She is the founder trustee and director of SPARROW (Sound and Picture Archives for Research on Women) in Mumbai.

A Purple Sea is a collection of 17 Tamil short stories presented in English Translation, translated by Lakshmi Holmstrom. The stories are arranged chronologically up to a point, and then several of later stories bear the same year, the year of publication of a collection of her stories in Tamil. Even so, journeying through the book is a journey in time and considerable challenge.

A Purple Sea is an event for Tamil readers and writers for another reason also. Contemporary Tamil writing does not often appear in print in competent translation and made available to discriminating non-Tamil readers. If one or two pieces do appear here and there, it seems more as a fulfillment of a representational obligation than out of appreciation of creative effort in Tamil. This becomes obvious when critics and reviewers either ignore the piece or go out of their way to run it down. It is certain that many self-respecting Tamil writers view with diffidence the representational efforts and don't feel happy with the condescending air of 'national' editors and anthologists.

To the reader accustomed to wide reading in English or any European language, this aspect will not appear very significant, as the body of feminist writing in English and other languages is very large and diverse, and far more vehement and aggressive than in *A Purple Sea*. But it is a very successful book. Lakshmi Holmstrom's introduction is a deft, measured effort in conveying the essentials of the writer and her fiction and in guiding the reader to derive a satisfactory literary experience of a world seen through the sensitive, thinking eyes of one who is unmistakably an artist.

A Purple Sea deserves to be treasured for its amazing gifts, each one hurting but also humanizing. The book is a resonant testimony to the empathy and loves which makes Lakshmi Holmstrom's English translation an intensely alive, creative experience. The stories are wide ranging in the nature of the protagonists, and in their agonies. Inevitably, most are about women in families, and even stories about single woman focus on her reaction to the male, to his institutions, even to his computers. Ambai explores many forms of oppression. The syntax of the Tamil language generally is so far from that of English that it is nearly impossible to give the flavor of the original in a translation. Lakshmi Holmstrom has intelligently refrained from attempting to do so. There is no awkwardness to distract our attention from the stories and their tellers.

Among the contemporary women writers Ambai and Mahasweta Devi occupy a prominent position in feminist writing with an immense insight into the workings of women psyche. As humanists they understand with a great insightful empathy the unfortunate predicament of many men. The literary works of these two writers are related to the continuous exploitation of women. Their novels describe women as every day warriors who gather stupendous strength from their loss, to fight back. The contribution of the writers to literature in general and to humanism in particular is commendable.

Mahasweta Devi and Ambai write in relation to the experiences with the people in their novels and stories. They are one among the rare writers who always aspire to find and explore something challenging without accepting the existing ideals and affected a new trend of writing in their regional language.

II
MYTH AS A MEDIUM

Myth is an inseparable component of the collective unconscious of the Indian mass. The national epics *The Ramayana* and *Mahabharata*, the regional folktales are never the stories of a distant past, but are inherent in everyday happenings. They dominate Indian culture strongly and powerfully and discuss all the major problems faced by the majority.

Victimisation and survival are the twin themes, which Mahasweta Devi and Ambai make use of in many of their works. Yet before exploring the concepts of victimization and survival, it is quite appropriate to analyze the concept of feminine vulnerability of how the female sex is prone by nature to make victimization.

Throughout history and in all civilizations, traits of women have been sought to be damaged and distorted, and her very status as a human being 'inferiorized' under the overwhelming male – domination. Sara Grimke comments, all history is 'male-centric' and she asserts that: Man has subjugated woman to his will, used her as a means to promote his selfish gratification, to minister to his sensual pleasure, to be instrumental in promoting his comfort, but never has he desired to elevate her to that rank she was created to fulfill. He has done all he could do to debase and enslave her mind; and now he looks triumphantly on the ruin he has wrought, and says, 'the being he has thus deeply injured in his inferior.

Kate Millet says, "The history of patriarchy presents a variety of cruelties and barbarities". The UN declaration on the elimination of violence against women defines violence as "that results in or is likely to result in physical, sexual or psychological or sentimentalism.

Ambai and Mahasweta Devi transcend the usual concerns of the feminist world and the relationships between man and woman. Their writing is involved with human rights of women and their fiction is a reflection of the violation of women rights and it includes: The act, omission or conduct by means of which physical, sexual or mental suffering is inflicted directly or indirectly, through deceit, seduction, threat, harassment, coercion, or any other means, on any woman with the purpose or effect of intimidating, punishing or humiliating her or of maintaining her in sex-stereo-typed roles, or of denying her human dignity, sexual self-determination, physical, mental and moral integrity or of undetermining the security of her person, her self-respect, or her personality, or of diminishing her physical or mental capabilities. Remember, Draupadi in *The Mahabharata* is a black woman. She must have been a tribal. In the state of Himachal Pradesh we still find the sort of fraternal polyandry that Draupadi was supposed to have practised in the Mahabharata. The polyandrous tribal women of Himachal Pradesh are said to belong to the Draupadi Gotra or clan. Among the south Indian tribals, Sita, the Queen of King Rama in the Ramayana, is not a human being. She is the wind in the grass; she is the flowing river, the fruit-yielding trees, the harvest to be gathered. She is nature.

The writers of today craft myth-like narratives that feature female heroes and world affirming mythic stories. For instance, Native American poet and novelist Louise Erdrich has twin heroes in her myth/novel *The Antelope Wife*, Chinese American writer *Maxine Hong Kingston* revives the myth of Fa Mulan, *The Woman Warrior*, and *Toni Morrison* has mythic tendencies in some of her work, like *Paradise*. Such works often involve feminist dimensions. Echoing Lévi-Strauss' image of the bricoleur, feminist myth scholar *Marta Weigle* agrees that perhaps the most important function of myth is its world-creating, world-affirming aspects. She distinguishes male-centred myths that often serve as charters for male dominance in society, from female-centred myths that typically affirm and create the world itself. It is thus very exciting to find so many strong women hero figures and re-visioned myths in the work of contemporary women writers.

Indian writers have drawn a considerable amount of its themes especially, feminism and nationalist themes from two major epics: *The Mahabharata* and *The Ramayana*. Like *The Bible* in European culture, these two major epics dominate Indian culture strongly and powerfully because they discuss all the major problems that are faced by all kinds of people, the issues of social inequality, and gender inequality of the lower class people.

Especially in India, for most of the people, myth is a lived reality, is a part of one's lived reality, every day existence, and large communities of people live by myths.

Throughout the history of civilization, the role and place of women has been distinct, and Ambai rewrites the role of women, denoting that women can be and should be the decision makers of their own lives. Mahasweta Devi demystifies the role of marginalised people, by articulating for the silenced voices of the tribal, subalterns and the outcaste. Devi brings the epic women characters like Kunti, Sita, Draupadi and the Nishadins into disturbing confrontations with the reader, compelling to see these women neither in scriptural contexts nor as patriotic rallying points, not even as women to be saved, but as representatives of the silenced and the invisible. By presenting the strength innate in each, Ambai and Devi construct a new world for modern young women.

Sita, the heroine of *the Ramayana* and Draupadi, the heroine of *the Mahabharata* have become signs or cultural icons as Pativratas (ideal wives) as earth born Goddess, in the epics and in the culture that influenced them, a woman alone, a woman the powerful, a woman capable of bringing shame upon her family is in need of control. On a relatively innocent level, she is viewed as a vulnerable creature in need of masculine protection. More insidiously, she is seen as essentially unable to control her own fatal force. But literary texts have brought subtle readings of these two epic women-Sita can wage a psychological war against her captor Ravana; Draupadi can argue.

The Mahabharata, attributed by Vyasa, is generally agreed to have been composed between 500 BCE to 400 CE. *The Ramayana*, attributed by Valmiki, is likely between 200 BCE to 200 CE. In the eleventh century, the Tamil poet, Kamban wrote a recension in the south, and in the sixteenth century, Tulsidas translated the epic into Avadi (old Hindu), which was later brought in to Bengali by Krittivasa,and into modern Hindi and William Jones translated in to English.

Both the epics recension of oral and written have emerged in all major Indian languages, as well as in European languages, from palm leaf to paper, drama, film, and poem. When one speaks of epic in India at large, with its literate and non literate audiences, no written text is necessary to mind: *The Mahabharata* or *Ramayana* is more likely to be envisioned. Doordarshan televised version of Ramayana, generally based on Tulsidas but incorporating other major texts, faithfully watched by over 80,000,000 viewers, some of whom bathed before watching, garlanded the set like a shrine, and considered viewing of Rama to be a religious experience.

Most of the versions of epics focus upon the traditional heroes (Rama in *the Ramayana*, the Pandava brothers in *the Mahabharata*); only very few versions focus on the views of the heroine. India is casted as Bharathmata, a maternal figure who has been captured, insulted, humiliated by evil men or rakshasas (demons) - Draupadi at the hands of Duryodhana, Sita at the hands of Ravana. Social activists or writers perceive the darkness and power of Sita and Draupadi to rescue from their avenging figure to a liberated one of a nation, of a gender, of a class.

The Mahabharata and *The Ramayana* has received a great deal of exegetical and explicatory attention over the years, yet the voices of the oppressed in the great epic have remained a somewhat neglected field of critical enquiry. Mahasweta Devi and Ambai's obvious intention is to underscore the contrast between the Rajavritta and Lokavritta, in which one honours and celebrates life. Kunti and Nishadin epitomise these two contrasting world views respectively.

After fifteen years of reign, Dhritarashtra, Gandhari, Kunti opt for a life of vanaprastha which is the third of the four stages of life prescribed tradition for a caste Hindu, the stage of abandoning worldly affairs. Much against his wishes Yudhistra lets them go. One day, as Dhritarashtra finishes his ablutions and returns to their hermitage, he comes to know that the forest has caught fire, the wind blows and the flames spread everywhere. The animals and the birds start deserting the forest, the blind Dhritarashtra, Gandhari with her blindfolded eyes and Kunti, all awaiting death, ready to give themselves up to the flames. They have spent their times in penance, prayers and yoga's till their death in the forest-fire.

In her attempt to amend the story, Devi has made a couple of brilliant interpolations - Kunti's confession, her guilt-stricken conscience at being unwed mother and her helplessness in not accepting Karna as her son in public, and greater crime committed by her, of which she was totally unaware, that is, the murder of six innocents belonging to the lower caste of society. In her introduction to the politics of literary theory and representation, Pankaj.K.Singh states that "this is an interrogative rewriting of a segment of the Mahabharata from the point of view of the Nishadin whose mother-in-law and her five sons were made die in the fire of lakshagraha to cover the escape of Kunti and her sons, and who holds up for interrogation the whole practice of rajavritta". Commenting upon its contemporary relevance Singh states further that "contemporary India has its own subalterns in the lower castes, the tribals, the landless, the poor and their women, Devi gives voice in her writing". Devi says, "it's my realisation that the more we read through the lines and give voice to the countless infantrymen used to protect the landed epical heroes, the dasis (mother of vidura, mother yuyutsu and countless others) and the 'vratyas' used as cannon fodder during Rajavritta emergency, the more the mythical time come into focus and the eternal game of politics comes into view".

The first thing which strikes us, as the story opens, is the pitiable, pathetic plight of Kunti, the mother of mighty Pandavas, queen of Pandu undergoes an existential despair, "Mother of the Pandava, wife of Pandu, the role of a daughter-in-law, the role of a queen, the role of a mother, playing these hundreds of roles where was the space, the time to be her true self? All that while, – amazingly – she never felt that anything was hers, hers alone".

She feels betrayed by life, "now, she can't bear to keep it all locked inside her". But never tried to learn the lifestyle of Nishadins, even though she did not care about their presence, "one day she sees some middle-aged Nishadins moving about the forest with their children and families... Kunti never tried to learn the language they speak". Kunti is not happy, she laments her present situation, whereas Nishadins are happy without any crumbling. After watching Nishadins' life Kunti feels that she has wasted her life by following the rituals of Rajavritta. "Watching Nishadins, it strikes her for the first time that she is wasting herself living like this, subsisting on rotting, withered leaves . Then realises that, "she never knew that she carried within her such a burden of unspoken thoughts".

Karna, one of the greatest heroes of *Mahabharata*, the son of Kunti was not accepted openly as her son because of the oppressive patriarchal social order gnawing away her conscience, "Karna looked so much at peace as he lay there, dead. Gandhari's piercing cry at the sight of Karna's body struck me like a whip. Why did I not have the courage? to cradle Karna's severed head in my lap and say, this is my first born? Dhananjaya! You have murdered your eldest brother! The son I abandoned for fear of public shame! Had I not disowned him, my name would have been sullied forever. Karna is the only one of my sons whose father I took of my own free will. What irony! What irony! Not one of the five Pandavas as sired by Pandu! Yet they are Pandavas. And Karna? A carpenter's son. O! Ancient mother! That day Kunti stayed silent. What greater sin can there be? Gandhari knew she was pure and innocent. This knowledge gave her courage to publicly speak the truth".

Death is approaching slowly towards her and she feels the urge to unburden herself before she dies. She knows that the confession at this stage is urgent because silence would be unpardonable. Then, her second confession, it's about when she directly went to Karna asking him to leave Duryodhana and join Yudhisthira, "I hesitate no more. I have not committed just one sin, after all. I had not told my sons about the birth of Karna. Then, the day before the battle, I went to Karna and told him, "abandon Duryodhana, side with Yudhisthira". At this time she feels for being Rajavritta, "living in the Rajavritta makes one cunning, treacherous". As love did not force Kunti to meet Karna only her self-interest did.

Against the world of Rajavritta, the world of Lokavritta, the world of Nishadins that is guided by nature's law, where different standards of judgments do not have any place. "Nature's law. Nature abhors waste. We honour life. When a man and woman come together, they create a new life. But you won't understand".

As the Nishadin proudly tells Kunti,"We do not deny the demands of life. If we are widowed we have the right to remarry. Those who wish to, can marry again. We did so. We have husbands, children... an eye for an eye, a tooth for a tooth that is the way of the Rajavritta. That is what Kurukshetra was all about. The Lokavritta's ways are different".

The conversation between Kunti and Nishadin brings out the sharp contrast between the worlds of Lokavritta and Rajavritta, "the Rajavritta folk and the Lokavritta folk have different values, different ideas of right and wrong. If a young Nishadin girl makes love to the boy of her choice and gets pregnant, we celebrate it with a wedding".

After the conversation Kunti understands clearly that Lokavritta's moral and spiritual ethics have been destroyed by the Rajavritta and which does not allow her to lead an instinctive life and to confess her sin. It is in the forest Kunti realises her true self, "do not forgive me, o mother! The brute wealth of the royal palace, the might of the son on the throne, I felt caged and torn to pieces".

Kunti dreams of her past life, being as Rajavritta, the life was so different, and had so many roles to play. Deep in the forest she notices the Nishadins but nothing registers on her mind, "oh, yes, I not only understand it, I speak it too. Of course you never thought of us as human, did you? No more than mute rocks, or trees, or animals".

Her conversation with the Nishadin made her realise that they are such self-composed, hardworking, innocent people, whereas Rajavritta knows only to attend the Brahmins and worship the Gods. Kunti does not remember ever talking to lower-class people, "How could they? Her life had been the Rajavritta, the Gods, serving the Brahmins. Has she ever spoken to a dasi? Has she developed any genuine bond with hidimba? Life outside the Rajavritta had not touched her at all".

Kunti wishes to confess the sins that she had committed. After every confession Kunti finds herself at peace, 'cleansed light' and on every occasion, the Nishadins hear her maternal lamentations, but Kunti believes them to be as dumb as rocks. Nishadins do not know her language or Kunti theirs; still the elderly Nishadins reprimand her,"no confessing of sins today? You... you... I've heard you out day after day, waiting to see if you will confess your gravest sin. Your language... likes mine...? Oh yes, not only understand it, I speak it too. Of course you never thought of us as human, did you? No more than the mute rocks or animals".

Kunti is astonished to know that the elderly Nishadin understands her language. The elderly Nishadin accuses her of committing the most heinous crime, "the massacre of innocents for self-interest". As the Varanavata episode from the Mahabharata was a conspiracy to kill Pandavas. But the Pandavas became acquainted with the plan of Kauravas and hatched a counter-plan for survival. When the vax palace was set on fire by the trusted soldiers of Duryodhana, the Pandavas escaped through a secret tunnel. In order to make the Kauravas believe that Kunti and Pandavas were burnt to death, an elderly Nishadin and her five sons were invited for a feast and oceans of wine were served with food. The innocent Nishadin and her five sons drank too much and dozed well. Kunti is shocked by this revelation and fears for her life. The elderly Nishadin makes a clear stance of their (tribal) ethics to Kunti, and says that she is not going to kill her.

The Nishadin informs Kunti that a forest fire, which is a disastrous natural phenomenon, has already broken out. She says, "Yes, we can tell, from smelling the air, just as the other creatures of the forest can, that a fire has started. That is why they are fleeing – like we are. Where to? Far away, beyond the reach of the forest fire. Where there are mountains, lakes and winding rivers".

Kunti asks for forgiveness but the elderly Nishadin says, "Three blind, weak and infirm people cannot make it there. One is blind from birth, another has chosen to be a blind and you, and you are the blindest of the three".

The thought of forest fire makes Kunti fearful but the Nishadin is not ready to forgive her. She believes that it is easy for the Rajavritta to commit sin, "to beg forgiveness is typical of the Rajavritta". The narrative ends with Kunti's acceptance of the destiny with the sense of finality."She got up. She has to go back to the Ashram. Wait for the forest fire. Dhritarashtra and Gandhari, after their loss of a hundred sons, are waiting patiently for death, waiting for the final fire to consume them. Kunti also welcomes death".

In the story *The Five Women* the narrators are five war widows, their husbands, foot soldiers, who died in Kurukshetra war to protect the "chariot – mounted" heroes. "These women are not of the Rajavritta, women of royalty, nor are they servants or attendants. These women are from the families of the hundreds of foot-soldiers – Podatics – from various other little kingdom".

The women of Rajavritta strictly follow the ordeal but the women of Janavritta live life in close association with the natural world. The Rajavritta is represented by Kunti, Draupadi, Subhadara and the pregnant Uttara whereas the five women from the Kurunjugal represent the Janavritta."I am Godhumi. This is Gomathi, holding my hand. That is Yamuna, with the red spot between her brows. That one standing there with a finger on her chin is Vitasta. And this is Vipasha, Vitasta's sister".

The five women consider the war as a futile clash of egos, "so many great kings joined in a war between brothers. Some choose one side, some cross over to the other. It was not just brother slaughtering brother. We know of quarrels – jealousies – rivalries too. But such a war for just a throne? This, a holy war?! A righteous war?! Just call it a war of greed!".

The five women are appointed to keep Uttara accompanied and help her to overcome her grief, but to Uttara all the five women seem to be inseparable. "The five women seem to think as one. They are so close that they seem to understand each other without words, and speak to one another with their eyes alone. They look, they understand".

The companionship of these five women is in contrast to the isolation of the women of the Rajavritta. Uttara feels as a stranger to them, she, like the other women of Rajavritta believes that all the soldiers who died in the holy war are much secured in Divyalok – the heaven, but the five young women reject this idea. Godhumi says, "no chariots came down from Divyalok. They did not go to heaven. The foot soldiers died fighting in the very same Dharmayudha. But no funeral rites were held for their souls".

Further they reject the idea of Dharmayudha, "this was not our Dharmayudha. Brother kills brother, uncle kills nephew, shishya kills guru. It may be your idea of dharma, it is not ours".

The Janavritta women enjoy the public participation whereas it is denied to Rajavritta. Thus Uttara expresses surprise, "imagine men and women singing together". The Rajavritta women have no companionship or bond with their child, "At best her child will stay with her a year. After that, the wet nurses will take over its upbringing. Royal offspring are not raised by their mothers. Then will begin the prescribed rites and rituals, the self-denial, the penance".

So, this story clearly shows that the Rajavritta were restricted by false notions of high civilization. The natural human state is represented by the five Kurunjugal tribal women, whose life, ideas and quests are opposite to the destructive and sterile attitudes of the higher social order. "Uttara understands the difference and is not ready to leave them". But as widows of Rajavritta, all the women (widows) concern only for Uttara and not for the five young widows. Rajavritta women expect them to give a good company to Uttara because she may beget a son for the throne. "how anxious her mother-in-law is! Draupadi, Subhadara, all the others, are deeply worried. If Uttara bears a son, he will be a king". After becoming so close with the five people Uttara used to question, "did the Rajavritta – the royalty – ever care to know about the Janavritta – common humanity?" Through the story "The Five Women" Mahasweta Devi reveals to the reader the 'other' side of Kurukshetra war and the ingeniousness of Rajavritta women towards Lokavritta people.

The third story, *Souvali* focuses on the irreconcilability of the Rajavritta and the Janavritta. Souvali is a former handmaid who served Dhritarashtra and bore him a son named Souvalya; known as yuyutsu. Souvali, a woman from Janavritta is forced to send her son to the Gurugrigha at the age of five, not able to bear the life of Janavritta, gives up her dasi status and lives outside of the town, waiting for her son to return.

Souvalya is insulted and discriminated against by the Kauravas, "Dasiputra! Slave child! It's because of this Dasiputra that you got water from a son's hand! Kunti! Gandhari! Gandhari never once, in all these years, acknowledged you as a Kaurava". But he only performs the last rites (tarpan) for Dhritarashtra after the forest fire.

The conversation between mother and son reveals that Souvalya is happy to rise above the status of dasi-putra by the Pandavas. But his mother is not happy to accept the recognition, rather she calls it a farce. She wants her son to be a Janavritta, "her son is foolish. Following the norms and customs of royalty even though he is one of the common folk. She thinks to herself, if you must learn, learn from your mother. I was nothing but a dasi in the royal house-hold but here, amongst the common people, I'm a free woman".

This story shows the difference between the centre and the margins of society. "It's true. It's in the Janavritta, amongst the common people, that we are in touch with our natural emotions. Tenderness, caring, compassion, romance, love, anger, jealousy. But in the Rajavritta, you know how they keep such natural emotions strictly in check".

Thus, Mahasweta Devi's characters exemplify the twin problems of class and gender. Mahasweta Devi's a different story "Draupadi " concentrates on the major crisis of Draupadi's humiliation at hastinapura after Yudhistra has lost her in a game of dice.

Briefly *The Mahabharata* chronicles the ancestry and the escalating conflicts of two sets of the brothers, the Pandavas and the Kauravas, for rulership of the land. In most recension, Draupadi is born from the earth (although some have her emerging from the fire of her father's ritual sacrifice). Not long thereafter (she emerges as a young woman of marriageable age), her father arranges a swayamvara, a gathering of eligible men who compete for her hand in marriage. Arjuna, the third of the five Pandavas, wins, as she had hoped he would. But when he returns with his brothers to tell their mother the joyful news, their mother, thinking he has won some material goods, commands him to share his winnings with his brothers. As her word can never be taken back, Arjuna must share her, to the consternation of all.

Draupadi in turn marries all five Pandavas, Yudhistra, the eldest and wisest; Bhima, noted for his physical strength and tenderheartedness; Arjuna, the consummate warrior, friend of Krishna, and Draupadi's favourite; and the twins Nakula and Sahadeva, celebrated for their good looks. They devise an arrangement to eradicate jealousy: beginning with Yudhisthira, each brother has sole right of conjugal access to Draupadi for a year at a time, during which the other may not even accidently enter the marital bedroom. Draupadi bears a son to her husband.

Eventually, due to pressure exerted upon them by the king Dhritarashtra, the two sets of brothers reconcile, although mutual suspicion remains. In a move of anticipation, Dhritarashtra divides up the kingdom between the two sides of the family: half to the Pandavas and the other half to the hundred Kauravas, an arrangement most unsatisfactory to the Kauravas. The leading Kaurava, Duryodhana, arranges for Yudhisthira's horse sacrifice and coronation, followed by a ritual game of dice in which players are supposed to ceremonially lose to the new king in the Kauravas grand assembly hall. But Duryodhana sets his maternal uncle Sakuni, a master at dice, to play in his stead, and the loaded dice take away yudhistra's land, wealth and slaves. Yudhistra then stakes each of his brothers in turn, again losing each time. He stakes himself, and again he loses.

While the Pandavas, stand aside helplessly as slaves, Duryodhana demands that Draupadi be brought out of the women's hall, and sends a messenger to fetch her. Informed about what has just occurred, she asks whether Yudhistra lost her before or after he lost himself, and argues that one who no longer owns himself cannot own another to give up. She sends back the messenger. Another messenger is sent, and again returns. Finally, in frustration, Duhshasana himself goes to the women's hall; Draupadi tells him that she is unable to come to men's gathering. Ignoring her protestations, he drags her by the hair out to the assembly hall, where she pleads in vain with her husband's to help her, which they cannot act upon. A debate ensues, interrupted by Duhshanan's demanding that Draupadi be stripped, and Duryodhana laughingly patting his thigh to invite her to rest.

This humiliation in the assembly hall is Draupadi's central crisis, and is related in variable ways. Most recension shows her calling for Krishna to protect her; some show her merely as being jeeringly told to pray. In either case, a miracle occurs: as Duhshasana pulls at the cloth, Draupadi remains clothed: sari after sari appears, and ultimately, after pulling off hundreds of saris, Dushasana collapses, weary and confused. Dhritarashtra halts the proceedings and grants Draupadi two boons. She asks for the freedom of Yudhisthira and for that of the other Pandavas. The king grants freedom to everyone, and restores all of their possessions and land to the Pandavas. A second dice game ensues, which Yudhisthira again loses: the terms of the loss are that the Pandavas must go into exile for twelve years, remain in exile in disguise for another year, after which their half of the kingdom would be restored. Draupadi follows them in exile, and through their years away from the kingdom is more eager for revenge: Bhima fulfils his promise to break Duryodhana's thigh and to drink Duhshanan's blood.

A modification of the Mahabharata's assembly hall scene, Draupadi brings forward the struggle of a santal woman (black like the epic's Draupadi, for whom she has been named by her mother's master). A cadre in the Naxalbari rebellion, Draupadi, in the text referred as 'Dopdi' is ultimately captured by Senanayak, a Bengali army officer whose expertise in anthropology makes him perfect for the task of apprehending tribals. "In order to destroy the enemy, become one".

Senanayak has become one just as in the Mahabharata, Kauravas planned to wipe out Draupadi's husband, the five Pandavas. Both the narratives clearly show the struggle of less powered people at the hands of powered ones and the less powered people's wake of the powerful cheating. Similarly to the disempowering of the epic Draupadi's husbands, who, enslaved by the loss at the dice, cannot move, Dopdi's husband is murdered. "On one such search, army informant Dukhiram Gharari saw a young Santal man lying on his stomach on a flat stone, dipping his face to drink water. The soldiers shot him as he lay. As the 303 threw him off spread-eagled and brought bloody foam to his mouth, he roared 'Ma-ho' and then went limp. They realise later that it was the redoubtable Dulna Majhi ".

She refuses to fall into the army's trap by going to bend his body. "The problem is thus solved. Then, leaving Dulna's body on the stone, the soldiers climb the trees in green camouflage. They embrace the leafy boughs like so many great Gods pass and wait as the large red ants bite their private parts to see if anyone comes to take away the baby. This is the hunter's way, not the soldiers. But Senanayak knows that these brutes can't be dispatched by the approved method. So he asks his men to draw the prey with a corpse as bait. All will come clear, he says. I have almost deciphered Dopdi's song. The soldiers get going at his command. But no one comes to claim Dulna's Corpse".

Rather than lead her pursuers to capture other rebels, Dopdi lets her be caught, refuses to tell names. Unlike the epic Draupadi, whose sari flows out in endless profusion, she is stripped, "Draupadi Mejhen was apprehended at 6.53 PM. It took about an hour to get her to camp. Questioning took another hour exactly. No one touched her, and she was allowed to sit on a canvas camp stool. At 8.57 Senanayak's dinner hour approached, and said, make her. Do the needful, he disappeared".

The next day she is ordered to Senanayak's tent and offered a pot of water to slake her by-now overpowering thirst. But her response upsets all expectations, "Draupadi stands up. She pours the water down on the ground. Tears her piece of cloth with her teeth. Seeing such strange behaviour, the guard says she's gone crazy, and runs for orders. He can lead the prisoner out but does not know what to do if the prisoner behaves incomprehensibly.

So he goes to ask his superior".

Mahasweta Devi's Draupadi refuses to be clothed again. She forces the confrontation with her tormentors-letting them see exactly what they have done to her, refusing to futilely attempt to cover her. No Goddess will come to help her and no king will fight for her behalf. Senanayak is paralyzed at what he sees, "Draupadi stands before him, naked. Thigh and public hait matted with dry blood. Two breasts, two wounds. What is this? He is about to bark. Draupadi comes closer. Stands with her hand on her hip, laughs and says, the object of your search, Dopdi Mejhen. You asked them to make me up, don't you want to see how they made me? Where are her clothes? Won't put them on, sir. Tearing them. Draupadi's black body comes even closer. Draupadi shakes with an indomitable laughter that Senanayak simply cannot understand. Her ravaged lips bleed as she begins laughing. Draupadi wipes the blood on her palm and says in a voice that is as terrifying, sky splitting and sharp as her ululation, what's the use of clothes? You can stripe me, but how can you clothe me again? Are you a Man? She looks around and chooses the front of Senanayak's white bush shirt to spit a bloody gob at and says, There isn't a man here that I should be ashamed of. I will not let you put my clothes on me. What more can you do? Come on, counter me - come on counter me -? Draupadi pushes Senanayak with her two mangled breasts and for the first time Senanayak is afraid to stand before an unarmed target, terribly afraid".

In *The Mahabharata* Draupadi is dragged from her menstrual cycle into the assembly hall in one garment, the stained garment is a signifier that Dushasana is expected to understand. She is not to be touched, and she certainly is not to be brought to the view of men. She reminds him, but he mocks her and forces her to be in the hall.

Dopdi's signifiers of blood, in contrast, mark a rape and torture completed rather than forestalled. The soldiers and Senanayak are paralyzed rather than goaded like Dushasana into further action. Like the epic Draupadi, who decries the impotence of her husbands, Dopdi can find no man present within the camp. Ferociously, she defiles Senanayak with her blood-she spits on him with her bleeding mouth, and pushes him with her wounded breasts into his white shirt. Occupying his physical, forcing him to see her "made up", she shoves his own fear into his face. Unarmed, but threatens what the actions of the next hour may be.

In Dopdi's case, the insults she hurls at Senanayak and his men- which echo those that the "master narrator" Vyasa gave to the epic Draupadi in the assembly hall, and even her spitting and her pushing her wounded breasts against him, defiling her tormentor with blood, just as Vyasa's menstruating Draupadi cannot help but contaminate Dushasana when he sinks into violence. Despite the bungling of Senanayak's aid's enthusiasm over his discovery that Dopdi's "hende rambra kecje keche, Pundi rambra keche keche" is Mundari language, her message is ultimately received, Senanayak who could dispatcher in seconds, is frozen, in the eternal, suspended moment of the narrative's end, unable to act.

Akin to Mahasweta Devi, Ambai (C.S.Lakshmi) rewrites one of the episodes of the Ramayana and introduces a new twentieth century Sita to the readers.

In *The Ramayana*, when Sita is reunited with Rama, he demands her to prove her purity, and it is too much for her to bear, so she returns to the forest; Senthiru of Atavi too like Sita goes to the forest at end of her life, and enjoys the rhythm, love, music of nature.

Although *The Ramayana* was composed during the same general time frame as *the Mahabharata, the Ramayana* is set in an earlier mythical time, in the age of Tretayuga; its ending begins Dwapara Yuga, the era of *the Mahabharata*. Again as *the Mahabharata* in precise, Sita's life will be set forth in brief. As Draupadi's emergence from an altar fire, Sita's "birth" from a furrow in the earth is miraculous, and as with Draupadi, her parents arrange for a contest, at which Rama wins her. His brothers Lakshman and Shatrughan. Sons of his father's wife Sumitra, Sita's sisters Urmila and Shrutakirti; his brother Bharat, a son of his father's wife Kaikeyi, marries her cousin Mandavi: a multiple wedding, but one which leaves no one aghast.

After some time in their marital home, that of the young men's father, king Dasaratha, Rama, who is destined to become the crown prince, is banished as the result of a court intrigue led by Kaikeyi, who wishes to enthrone her son Bharat. Accompanied by Sita and Lakshman, Rama must live in the forest for fourteen years. The king dies of grief, and Bharat takes over the headship of the country, but puts Rama's sandals on the throne as a symbol of the "true" king while he and Shatrugna await Rama's return.

In their travels, the trio visits various stages and has many adventures of one sort of another: exile becomes idyll, until a Rakshasi (female demon) falls in love with Rama, attempts to kill Sita, and is mutilated by Lakshman. Complaining to her brother Ravana, she relates Sita's beauty – and Ravana, despite his 10,000 wives, falls in love with the thought of Sita, and determines to capture her for himself. He sends another demon in disguise of a golden deer adorned with jewels, which attracts Sita's attention. She sends Rama after it; it leads him far astray, but when he finally slays it with an arrow, it calls out Sita's name, in Rama's voice. Greatly upset, Sita insists that Lakshman go to his brother's aid; he suspects a ruse and refuses to leave. Now infuriated, Sita accuses him of having sexual desires on her, and demands him to go. Lakshman inscribes a circle, the Lakshmanrekha, around the house: no one other than him or Rama will be able to cross it if Sita does not stop over it.

With Lakshman out of the way, Ravana arrives at the house, disguised as a sage, and asks for refreshment. Sita steps across the line to bring him some water, and he apprehends her and abducts her in his aerial car to Lanka, his domain in the south. Although Sita is seemingly under his control, fate is on her side: Ravana lives under a cause that to attempt sexual intercourse with an unwilling woman will kill him (his 10,000 wives, many of whom he abducted, very much , refuses to have anything to do with him, and Ravana wages psychological warfare upon her, alternately cajoling and threatening. Sita wages war in return, eating only enough to stay alive, and refusing to wash, to change her clothes, or to otherwise beautify herself: making herself as thin and repellent as possible. Her virtues eventually endear her to the fierce Rakshas Is set to guard her, and she stubbornly holds her ground against Ravana. While this is transpiring, Rama and Lakshman, aided by the Vanara (Monkey) general Hanuman, ultimately locate her and fight Ravana to the death.

One would expect a perfect end at this point, and one would be surprised at what actually occurs: in front of the multitudes present, Rama rejects Sita, telling her that he fought this war for the sake of his honour, that she is now free to go anywhere: to one of his brothers, to a Rakshasa, to a monkey. Because she has lived in the home of another man (her unwillingness is irrelevant), her purity is called into question. At first, tears speak more eloquently for Sita than words, but she wipes her face, she commands Lakshman to build a fire: he looks to Rama for guidance, and then builds the pyre. Doing obeisance to Rama and entering the fire, she calls four times upon the flame as the witness to her purity: "If my heart has never strayed away from [Rama], may the God of fire, who sees all things in the world, protect me on all sides? If [Rama] wrongly judges me, who is innocent, as having misbehaved, may fire, the universal witness, save me from all danger. If I have never been guilty of transgression in thought, word or deed again at

[Rama]... may fire protect me! If the exalted Lord, the Sun-god, the Wind-god, the deities of the different directions, those presiding over day and night, and the twilight, the goddess earth and others know that I am blameless, may the fire do me no harm.

She emerges unharmed, resplendent – Valmiki's even adding that her garlands were still fresh, the sweat from her stress undired, after the Gods have proclaimed her spotlessness. The couple reconciles.

Kamban ends the narrative shortly thereafter, but in Valmiki's; Sita has more ordeals to endure. Not long after returning home to Ajodhya to reign in triumph, Rama, bowing to political pressures, commands Lakshman to abandon the now- pregnant Sita in the forest, presumably to die. While Lakshman must obey Rama, he took her instead to Valmiki's ashram, where she gives birth to twin sons, Lav and Kush, and presumably, given the customs of the time of writing, joins in the life of the religious community.

Years later, by coincidence, sons and father are reunited. Rama appears to have repented, and overjoyed that she is still alive, sends for Sita - but she must prove her purity yet once more. Seemingly having had enough of her husband's demands, Sita obliges him, but in a fashion obverse to the fire ritual: where as she had once called for the fire to burn her if she were impure, she now calls for her mother, the Earth to take her back if she is pure.If it is true that I have never so much as thought of any man other than, say the Goddess... open her door wide and take me to her bosom. If it is true that I have always worshipped Rama in thought, word and deed, May the Goddess-queen of Madhava open her door and accept me. If what I have said now is the truth, and I have never looked upon any one as greater than Rama, may the divine consort of Madhava give me entrance into her abode!The Earth opens, and the enthroned Goddess takes her daughter back into her lap, letting the ground close above them.

At this juncture, Ambai makes Sita realise her quest for self-realisation, liberation and equality. Like Sita, Ambai's Senthiru expects recognition from her husband and not recognized by him because she is a woman. She supports her husband's (Thirumalai) business and promotes it to an international level. But Thirumalai mindlessly excludes her from the new export business, so Senthiru feels hurt and leaves the family. Living close to nature in the nearby forest, she tries to seek peace of mind. She writes the story of Sita in the name of 'Sitaayanam'. She deconstructs the image of Rama as a monogamist divine man to depict him as a suspicious, jealous, proud, and selfish patriarch and asserts Sita's right to lead a single life. "Epic women went along with their husbands into forests. It is men who went into the forest alone— leaving their wife behind— to hunt or to wage war. (When the father instructed /ordered the son to be exiled). For, the woman becomes Sita to walk with her husband Rama when the father orders to exile. The state of the woman is Thamayanthi who walked with his Nalan to the forest. The state of a woman is like Rishi's wife with her Rishi husband. In case a woman wishes to go alone into the forest she may be the Menagai to disturb the penance. Or else forest will be bewilderment for a woman. And there should be a man beside her to protect. For a woman, forest is a punishment. To go to forest is a process like to weaken and to alienate her. This is how Thirumalai argued".

Senthiru gets the meaning of life only through music. She learns from a sanyasi, in the forest about the secret of life that just as music, whether carnatic or Hindustani, is the same to a peaceful mind, so is life everywhere. The voice of a cuckoo can be melodies to an ever-happy mind. To a troubled heart, everything seems problematic and troublesome.

At first, Thirumalai pokes fun at Senthiru's decision to leave the house and criticises her for the forest plan. He says that women have gone to the forest with their husbands in puranas and the animals and flowers in the forest have been hostile to them. But Senthiru is serious, gets the permission of the forest department, goes to the nearby forest and plans to rewrite the epic and purnas to get relaxation. "It was dawn, she felt like walking till her legs get tired and she wore her footwear. When she was about to leave her room, an attender appeared before her. She ordered me to bring some tea and sat on the stairs. It was all greens in different shades (dark green, light green, pale green)".

The forest department arranges a comfortable stay for her and gives information about the forest. In spite of repeated phone calls from her husband, she is too firm to stay in the forest and not ready to change her decision for anyone. While taking a walk she happens to meet three tribal women- Meenabai, Rukmani Bai and Savita Bhabhi. They discuss with her and share their food with her.

One day-light hour the three tribal women take Senthiru to their houses. Their husbands are away from home. They prepare food together and eat together. They also drink toddy. Senthiru is reminded of an occasion when she went to Murut- Janjeera Fort with friends and children. Senthiru was unexpectedly held up in the fort, and there was a sign of a storm so the boatman refused to take the boat. During that night, Senthiru tasted toddy and fish to overcome the coldness. Now, for the second time, she tastes toddy. Soon Senthiru and tribal women hear music from Veena at a distance. The tribal women tell her that one Soofi Baba living in hermitage plays Veena.

The following day, Senthiru goes to the hermitage. She talks with hermit about music. The hermit suggests to her that the choice is between two things- sanyasam and non sanyasam. She replies that she cannot live in Bombay... the hermit advises that she can enjoy the pleasure of the forest in Bombay. As the Baba explains, Senthiru understands that everything is on one's will. She walks towards her room with a clear mind.

Senthiru now attempts to write the most famous Indian Epic *The Ramayana*. "The time has come to rewrite the epics," she said, laughingly, after scribbling those lines on the palm leaf, there was a shade at the next moment. Sita raised her head to see and it was the sage Valmiki.What are you writing to my child? Uttered he.Stood up praising him and exclaimed expedition of Sita's travel.Isn't the Ramayana that I wrote enough? Exclaimed Valmiki. No for the next ages there will be many Ramayana's, many Rams, and many Sita's. Picked the palm leaves in his hands and exclaimed "isn't this my written Sita?".

She makes Sita as the central figure in the story *Sitaayanam* and narrates the feelings, thoughts, and experiences of Sita in *Sitaayanam* from Sita's point of view. Her story ends with Sita living alone, leaving her children to Rama and abandoning the security of Valmiki's ashram to wander deep into the forest. There, following the sounds of vina music to a small hut, she encounters an ascetic who identifies himself as Ravana. When he tells how he escaped death and has waited meeting her again, exasperated Sita assumes he is still in thrall to his infatuation with young Sita. Announcing that she is over forty years old, she expresses weariness with her life's many tragedies" and resentment at being imprisoned in her body. Yet Ravana too has aged, and now devotes himself to music. He offers to teach Sita to play the Rudravinai, a stringed instrument whose design is inspired, according to tradition, by the shape of Parvati's body. Although Ravana concedes that the body can act as a prison, he contends that it can be a path to fulfilment if used to make music. He urges her to learn the Rudravinai so creativity can fill her life: "Don't think of it as an ordinary musical instrument. Think of it as your life, and play on it". When he attempts to put the instrument in her lap, Sita instead insists that he place it on the ground so she can grasp it herself. When asked why, she describes herself as one with "a life that many hands have tossed about, like a ball. Now let me take hold of it [the vina];

take it into my own hands".

Imagining her heroine as an older woman in Ambai's day, Ambai imputes to Sita a version of amid-life reassessment. Like today's "empty nesters," Sita's responsibilities for her offspring have largely ended. Looking back on many years of self-sacrifice, Sita sees how she let others control her life. The tragedies she suffered have drained and disheartened her, but Ravana's offer suggests a new chance. Lifting the Rudravinai, as if reconnecting with her own body (the body of a Goddess), she embraces a form of creative expression not available to her earlier. Ambai provides a fresh way of thinking about Sita, through the prism of middle age. Ambai rewrites not only the story of Sita, but also the portrayal of Hindu asceticism in the forest. In the conversation between Sita and Ravana, Sita talks of imprisonment in the body, articulating the view that one goes to the forest to burn off desires and attachment to pleasures. Instead of instructing Sita to isolate herself and burn off desires, however, Ravana urges her to study music. In Ambai's forest, Sita does renounce her previous status as a princess and submit herself to the teachings of a guru. Her focus, however, is not traditional yoga but mastering the vina. Rather than mortify the body, she uses it to express herself through music. Distance from everyday worldly affairs of the city allows a person in the forest the opportunity to shape one's own life, after a lifetime of attending constantly to the needs of others, according to Ambai.

The story, *The Sitaayanam* breaks the traditional myth of Rama's divinity and presets him as an ordinary man who cannot understand the feelings and thoughts of their better-half. The story Atavi ends with a peace of mind attained by both Senthiru and Sita.

Ambai has divided the story into an unequal twelve parts, by following the parallel pattern Ambai describes the lives of two women - one belonging to epic age and another modern age. She portrays that the condition of women has been the same and women have to take bold steps to design their own lives. Forest becomes the common locale for both the heroines and Senthiru's life too becomes another *sitaayanam*.

Marked by successive waves of political upheaval before and after independence, the twentieth century has witnessed recasting after recasting of epic heroines, 'individual' characters emblematic of India struggling against British domination, 'collective' heroines bound up in the disputed land, and re-representations of the 'underground Sita'. By exploring the changing inscriptions of Sita and Draupadi (of mythic times and modern), in bringing out the subversive aspects of female characters often dismissed as saintly, as submissive, as self-effacing or in the rare instances of their self-assertion, as capricious, insane, or dangerous.

Mahasweta Devi and Ambai end the text, dystopian as it is in general, on a note of hope. After the long struggle to overcome the obstacles of caste and gender, the protagonists of both texts can look forward to at least the possibility of fulfilment, as they define it. The stories are concerned with the exploitation of women and survival, crossing of boundaries and challenging norms in a male-dominated culture. The authors question the male authority, the masculine and feminine stereotypes, by revealing the contradiction between the unconscious desire and conscious reality experienced by women everyday in the society.

Thus, Kunti, Sita and Draupadi of Mahasweta and Ambai are brought into disturbing confrontations with the reader, to see them not in scriptural contexts, not as patriotic rallying points, not even as women to be saved, but rather as represent actions of silenced and invisible who now demand to be seen and heard. The writers by presenting the strength inherent in each, they construct a new world for modern young women. And especially, they show that the subalterns, those of the lowest strata of Indian society have recoverable voices, than the scholars.

III
THE SCREAM OF SILENCE

The position and identity differentiate as privileged and marginalized, oppressor and oppressed, or ruler and subject. Individuals who are not recognized in any part of the human world with their level of consciousness and unheard voices are the issue of the silent.

"If I work in drama... I'll do it for my people..." Mahasweta Devi explains the commitment of a writer. Mahasweta Devi and Ambai are one among the few writers in India with an unflinching commitment and passion for the urban and the rural exploited class. Unlike the writers who revel in pleasing the middle and upper classes by "weaving narcissistic fantasies in the name of literature". Mahasweta Devi and Ambai, fascinated by the socio-economic history of human life, take a stand "in defense of the exploited. Otherwise history would never forgive (her/him)". They seek to resurrect older periods in history in their immediate physicality, as if they are nothing less than contemporary. They think that social evils are an off-shoot of the present social system, and desire a radical transformation of it. In her introduction to Agnigarbha (1978) a collection of her long stories, Mahasweta Devi writes: "After thirty one years of Independence, I find my people still groaning under hunger, landlessness, and indebtedness, and bonded labour... All the parties... have failed their commitment to the common people. I do not hope to see in my lifetime any reason to change this conviction of mine. Hence, I go on writing to the best of my abilities about the people ".

Subalternity could be analyzed as marginalized or 'other' figures as their essence is under shadow, they are not visible in the space of center or main stream. In this context they grow with their own stories and narratives which collaboratively build their values. It is reflected in their manner of acceptance and the collective consciousness in regard to their social position. Mahasweta Devi's *Standayani, Old Women, Rudali* and Ambai's *A Kitchen in the Corner of a House (Veettin moolayil oru samaiyalarai), A Deer in the Forest(Kattil oru man)* and *Unpublished Manuscript (Prasurikkappatatha Kaippirathi), Sirakukal Muriyum* are the text to refer and justify the mode of subaltern female identity.

The two significant positions that dominate the society's understanding about women are that of the role of a wife and of a mother. In Indian culture, the daughters of a family marry and move into their husbands' houses, which include their entire families. Daughters-in-law manage households and provide heirs to the families. For the growth of the human race, God gifted women with the unique power to give birth whilst bringing a new life into this world. Pregnancy, childbirth and motherhood are some of the sex-specific roles that are assumed to be an essential part of every female's development. Without attaining motherhood a woman's persona remains hollow. During pregnancy, the child is connected with the mother through the umbilical cord which is the medium of nourishment for the child. It's the mother who initiates the child's journey in this amazing new world, gives him or her food, provides the child with lessons, exposes him or her to true-life, answers all their queries, helps them discover their roots and teaches them the art of living. Motherhood, the term is not only confined to the "biological mother" but also connected with the "surrogate mother", "legal mother" and "Nurturing mother". Motherhood in Indian society crowns a woman with an honored status not in the sense of special right but as an attribute without which she is looked down on. In the context of a mother and the nation, a nineteenth century Swedish writer, Ellen Key says: "The Mother is the most precious possession of the nation, so precious that society advances its highest well-being when it protects the functions of the mother." Mahasweta Devi attacks the silence that surrounds the social-political-cultural issues, and through her narrative on "Jashoda", focuses on the experience of motherhood and also on the exploitation of women which remains unobserved otherwise.

Breast Trilogy: The story of Jashoda demonstrates the theme of commodification of mother's milk; it is the first true story in the *Breast*

Trilogy, the other two being *Draupadi* and *Behind the Bodice: Choli Ke Piche*. *Breast-Giver* is prominently rich in its encrusted complexity and concentration on the same theme.

A preoccupation with the women figure in a number of her stories outlines another dimension of Mahasweta Devi's engagement with gender. In this subaltern location, females are having their position within the boundary of their family needs and survival forces. The female modes differ for locating the female identity. They grow with their power of resistance as they use their bodily performative acts as means of devaluing the power's existence. Spivak uses the *Breast Stories* of Mahasweta Devi to explain the position and real existence of females in the context of the unheard situation of the group. Jashoda in Mahasweta Devi's story, *Standayani* makes her presence and existence as a breast feeder and a source of survival for her paralyzed husband. They grow with the strength of resisting the power politics without revolt. In this mode female struggle and resistance, feminism gets different outlook.

Jashoda belongs to an economically weak class. She adopts the profession of wet nurse to support her family when her husband Kangalicharan gets crippled in an accident. To support her family she feeds twenty children. Though this new employment forces her to be repeatedly pregnant, yet it gives her social and political significance in the form of "Mother of the world".

In the present story, the breast is the source of food and livelihood for Jashoda's family. The Haldar household was using Jashoda's body. Jashoda is paid to breastfeed many children of her master and mistress, her abundant milk becomes a vehicle of income for her husband and family. Jashoda is exploited as a woman as well as of the class structure, the change of time and situation. It's only the difference of class that the upper class women of Haldar family pay lower class Jashoda for breast feeding their children in order to escape from ruining their gorgeousness. The Haldar household takes advantage of the fact that she is poor and that God chose motherhood as a profession for Jashoda. Jashoda dies a lonely death due to breast cancer. When she is no longer 'useful' for her friends and relatives, they abandon and forget her.

Devi says: "Jashoda's good fortune was her ability to bear children. All this misfortune happened to her as soon as that vanished. Now is the downward time for Jashoda the milk-filled faithful wife who was the object of reverence of the local houses devoted to the holy mother".

The concept of wet nurse is a rarely explored concept in the literature. In the very opening of the story Jashoda is introduced as: "Kangalicharan's wife from birth, the mother of twenty children, living or dead, counted on her fingers. Jashoda doesn't remember all when there was no child in her womb, when she didn't feel faint in the morning, when kangali's body didn't drill her body like a geologist in a darkness lit only by an oil lamp. She never had the time to calculate if she could or could not bear motherhood". Motherhood was always her way of living and keeping alive her world of countless beings. Jashoda was a mother by profession, professional mother. When her breasts get affected with cancer with which she fed, the infants mock at "her with a hundred mouths and hundred eyes".

The endless sacrifices that Jashoda made returned her nothing but suffering alone in silence. Jashoda in her innocence feels that all around her are milk sons: "Who's looking? Are these her own people? The people whom she suckled because she carried them, or those she suckled for a living? Jashoda thought, after all she had suckled the world, could she then die alone? The doctor who sees her every day, the person who will cover her face with a sheet, will put her on a cart, will lower her at the burning ghat, the untouchable who will put her in a furnace, all are her milk-sons".

Wretchedly, Jashoda leaves the world silently burdened with the pain of having none of her "own" attending to her in the last stages of her life, is a burden, oppression, and the reason for exploitation. The story of the *Breast Giver* brings to the surface, the gloomy reality of the process of sanctification of motherhood. Jashoda becomes a "Milk mother" for the Haldar family and dies suffering alone in silence due to breast cancer. In spite of so many children, she receives a lonely cremation by the hospital staff. As long as she remained fertile, the exploiters were happy with her produce and the moment she got cancer, they abandoned her. Thus Mahasweta Devi shows how the "Milk mother" pays a heavy price for her ignorance and dies of severe pain. She exposes the hidden exploitation of a poor woman, a faithful wife and a great mother, Jashoda.

The second story *Old Women –Statue and The Fairy Tale of Mohanpur* Mahasweta Devi criticize the life of the downtrodden and the tribal communities in India. In the story, *Statue*, Mahasweta Devi's delineation of the protagonist Dulali is heart- rending. Dulali is a decrepit old woman of seventy- eight years age who has been condemned as a witch and outcast both in her home and in the village, "rather than kill her physically they kept her in a room raised on the yard's far side". Her only sin was that, belonging to the Bhunya Tribe, widowed at the age of six she fell in love with Dindayal of the Thakur family – a Brahmin. The novelist uses the flashback technique to ground us in the present, passed through the reminiscence of Dulali, her memory of what happened fifty years ago. The past does not matter to her anymore, she believes in her present and dreams only about food: "in her dream she wears a whole cloth and eats a full serving of rice in a bell- metal plate. Every day, only rice, no lentils. No vegetables. Only rice".

At this age, she is not sad over past happenings but obsessed with the immediate problem of hunger. The cast- duty cross fire ruins the life of Pishi, it is a many layered tragedy like "multiple destructions with one explosion". Dulali a woman, a widow, an outcast is the silent sufferer of the pain inflicted on her, both by the village and the family.

The story *Statue* poignantly portrays how Dulali is preoccupied with filling her stomach and surviving from a day today. In the second story *The Fairy Tale of Mohanpur,* the protagonist Andi loses her eyes through a combination of poverty, societal indifference and governmental apathy, even as she persists in her belief in fairy tale solutions. Old Andi always dreams of a fairytale where there is, "Old Andi alone knows the fairytale of Mohanpur. In which fairy tale there are paddy stacks in every house, and cows in every cowshed. In that fairy tale Behula is a flowing river. Whenever the fisherman casts his net in that river, silvery fish come up as the harvest of the water. In that fairy tale there is no starvation, no famine, no despotism from Hedo Naskar, none of the unbearable suffering of the sharecropper, no disease, no decrepitude. Old Andi hasn't seen the Mohanpur of fairy tale with her own eyes. Her ancestors hadn't either. That Mohanpur did not exist in reality. When Behula changed its course, it went under water".

But the real Mohanpur is a place where poverty is complete. Though old Andi is a mother of four sons, with dim eyesight, she slaves for her belly's sake because whatever her sons bring is just enough to buy rice. The preoccupation with the tummy is the predominant leitmotif of the story. Andi's blindness unravels the corrupt social and political system in Mohanpur. When Andi is taken to the Irkanpur Health Centre, we learn that the place is a symbol of the degenerate state of affairs at every level. There is only one doctor serving as many as 60 patients, only 20 beds, where there is a kitchen but no cook. "Andi comes to the hospital sitting on straw. The Irkanpur Health Centre is unable to bear the health requirements of this Behula Block. The population of the Behula Block villages is 7,051.

There are 20 beds at the Health Centre hospital, on the average there are 60 patients at any given time. It is a daily sight to see more than one patient to a bed, patients strewn on the floor. Twenty beds cannot justify two doctors, this is the doctor-in-charge grasped long ago. It is not possible for him alone to prescribe the procedure for the malaria, cholera, worms, blood dysentery, dropsy, tuberculosis-typhoid, pneumonia, encephalitis- anaemia, diabetes, gastric ulcer, cuts-body blows- burns-snake-bite, mad dog or fox bite- ear infection- diphtheria, etc. that afflict the bodies of the average 100 outdoor and 60 indoor patients, debilitated and resistance-less as they are with malnutrition".

The groceries are supplied on contract by Hedo Naskar, the only rich man and a political bigwig of Mohanpur. Naskar, whose only intention is to make money, is not known for his honesty. He deceives the government and the people. Ironically the hospital in Andi resembles heaven. She says to her grandson: "Groceries are supplied by Hedo Naskar. The temporary cook takes a cut out of the supplies. The patients are happy with an apology for food! There is never any disinfectant, cotton wool or bandage. In an emergency the doctor boils his instruments and lights a hurricane lantern to operate. Why should it be a surprise that both the compounder Hari Nandi and the peon Enayet examine patients? Knowing all, Enayet asks Andi to come. Andi and Nodo wait for a long time. Andi shakes her head constantly. This Health Centre seems to her an astonishing heaven. She says to her grandson, great if I get in once. A bed to lie on, a belly full of food. Ouf, What a lot of convenience Nodo".

The visit of the specialist to the hospital exists only on paper. The old woman had to bribe Enayet, the peon, for even a visit to the doctor. She is treated for cataract with just eye drops. She thinks she is cured and can see everything clearly.

Gobindo, Andi's nephew and a party activist, is a contrast to Hedo Naskar, is a community health worker known for his honesty. He sincerely works for the upliftment of his society, forcibly takes boys and girls of the village and puts them in school. Gobindo believes in education which will later help them to progress in life and fight for their rights. He strives hard to drive into villagers that Hedo Naskar is exploiting them. He helps them to get their wages and fair share of their rice. It is he who discovers that the doctor at the health centre has erroneously treated Old Andi. He learns that Hedo Naskar is responsible for no specialist visiting the hospital. He dares to question Naskar "if a good medicine comes, it has to come to you. Whatever the pharmaceuticals give, you take away, is it only trade? Can one always look for profits?".

Gobindo succeeds in arranging for the district doctor to check old Andi's operation. Her nephew Gobindo is her only ray of hope. The villagers at first resist the instigation of Gobindo to fight the injustice met out by Naskar. But gradually they place more faith in him, allowing them to win their battle. It remains to be seen whether he truly transforms the village life, their attitude, backwardness, their poverty and hunger. His goodness is limited in that it goes only as far as fixing old Andi's operation. To Andi on the other hand, she stops worrying about the fate of her eyes: "She has been admitted at the hospital. She will eat all kinds of things at the hospital, the doctor will come again from the district town, Everything is just like a fairy tale one by one! She mutters, amazed, her face in the depths of this fairy tale ravine looks most fulfilled".

Mahasweta Devi delicately draws a tender and sensitive picture of the two old women caught in the socio-political system of oppression within which they are forced to survive. The political history is deeply interwoven with the private lives of the individuals in order to draw a social comment, a philosophy. In *Rudali*, the novella presents the static, unchanging pastoral corrupt system of dominant classes and castes and the exploitation of the lower classes and castes. Mahasweta Devi, at the beginning of the novel, places her central character Sanichari in the arena of low-caste poverty. The problems of Sanichari are also the problems of her caste, class and her gender. Unlike any romantic writer the author is hardly interested in portraying the physical appearance of the central characters.

Further, the author concentrates more on the pangs of the female protagonist who echoes the agonies of other female characters. In fact, Sanichari belongs to the social marginality which remains far off from the socio-cultural and economical focus. Her marginality becomes graver as she is a female, and is further dominated by the males of her own caste and community. Religion further impoverishes and enclave causing indebtedness through its web of demand and obligations.

The author brings together have and have not on the same path for neglecting their responsibilities of nourishing their old relatives. Poor do not have money to spend for the medicinal treatment of their relatives, where as aristocratic have plenty of money, but unwilling to spend a single paisa for the treatment of their old relatives. There is a competition among the rich fellows to spend huge amount on the death ceremonies of their relatives only for the sake of gaining prestige.

Dulan becomes a guiding star for Sanichari in every occasion of her life. After Bikhni's death Sanichari is under pressure to leave to work as Rudali, Dulan understand the gravity of situation and says to Sanichari, "Look Budhua's ma, it is wrong to give up one's land and your profession of funeral wailing is like your land you must not give it up". Community is a medium of offence for the exploiters at the same time it becomes the form of protection and strength for the exploited.

The writer stresses on the importance of community for the weaker section of the society, the community bondage between the poor and oppressed is strong enough for survival of each and all of the community. There are a number of examples depicted in the novel by the author how the poor and oppressed help and work together in their respective communities. The author portrays with examples that the marginalized men and women help and support each other, on the contrary the upper caste and class people take advantage of and betray their relatives for gaining wealth, money, land, and property. It is impossible for the marginalized people to survive in the village without the support of each other. The author presents the central character Sanichari working very hard beside her husband, her son and her grandson to support her family for survival and livelihood. Sanichari and her childhood playmate Bikhni are abandoned by their family, accepted by the bondage of community and friendship. Mahasweta Devi explores the theme of twice marginalized sector of community blamed as prostitutes. Dulan blames the money lenders are responsible for the increasing number of prostitutes in the villages. The landlords physically used the young women of the low caste and discarded them after their need was over just like use and throw. Some of them even beget children from such women but reject their responsibilities as a parent. Some women run away from their homes and accepted unwillingly the profession of prostitute for better option of livelihood, these women becomes prostitute for the sake of feeding their stomach and save them from starvation. The young women of the village having no clothes, no food and no self-respect turn towards the profession of prostitution. Neither the prostitutes don't earn enough to fulfill their stomach nor do they regain their self respect. The text revolves around the issue of prostitute, the daughter-in-law of Sanichari escapes from poverty ridden existence leaving behind all her duties and responsibilities even her small son, driven by hunger and need in excess of what her daily life can offer. Prostitutes is also an outcome of exploitative system of rich people, prostitutes are the victims of these social,political and economical system which is used by the aristocratic male society.

The text of *Rudali* highlights the bond ageing relation between women, the relation between Sanichari and Bikhni is of course close, sensitive, affectionate and supportive. Sanichari meets Bikhni in the marketplace, where she is searching for her grandson who is already lost; she is free from all other ties and relations. On the other hand Bikhni is equally abandoned by her son; leave her home with no plan about where to go. She prepares to survive by begging at some railway station if necessary. In every domain of life such as social, financial, caste, gender, age, family these women are tribally equal .Bikhni is delighted with Sanichari's house, she loves a household work, she cleans the house, clothes, mats and quilts, she fetches water from the river and with little effort start vegetable patch in front of Sanichari's house. The dreams of the marginalized people are very simple, straight forward and ordinary, but these dreams are never fulfilled. The central character of the novel, Sanichari has a simple dream to live peacefully in the bosom of her family surrounded by the grand-children, she desires to buy a wooden comb for her hair, to wear bangles for a full year, neither of her dreams are materialized. Her aspiration of sharing a bowl of gud and sattu with her grandson in the winter season is unfulfilled. Even another important character in the novel Bikhni has a very simple desire to meet her son in one of her relatives' marriage is never fulfilled. The author devotes much of the text to tracing evolution into a professional team; she also insists that this is a story of survival. The major concern of the text is to establish itself, as reality and not as fiction.

The harsh realities of poverty, exploitation, the struggle for survival and deaths are exposed in the brutal detail by the writer in the novel. The gender issues are secondary as discourse of class in the text. The patriarchy is also no more dominant factor in the text, the male characters in the novel specially relatives' to Sanichari fade away from her life one by one. Her husband passed away by drinking sour milk which is used for cleaning the idol of lord Shiva. Her loving and hard working son Budhua passed away due to the dangerous disease tuberculosis .Sanichari's son Budhua is a sensitive, thoughtful, gentle carving both to his mother and his wife. Her grandson Haroa also run away from her house leaving behind old, lonely woman. There is only one man from her community who helped her whenever she needed his advice, at the beginning Dulan advices Sanichari, "... pick up a nice stone from the banks of Kuruda river. And anoint it with oil and sindor and proclaim that Mahabirji had come to me in my dreams. ...collect offerings form the devout".

He also gives a suggestion to Sanichari that, "Look here, Buddha's ma, there's no bigger god than one's belly". For the belly sake everything is permissible. Ramji Maharaj said so. Finally he tells them to become Rudali just to wail and cry and accompany the corpse to get food, clothes and thus survive.

Mahasweta Devi at the closing of the text comprised the marginalized and the outcaste intervening to the center of the society. The writer throughout the text represented the marginalized voices through central and other various characters.

Ambai's *A Kitchen in the Corner of a House (Veettin moolayil oru samaiyalarai), A Deer in the Forest (Kattil oru man)* and *Unpublished Manuscript (Prasurikkappatatha Kaippirathi)* plot around the major feminine concerns such as survival, conflict, freedom, identity and motherhood. Male authority in a patriarchal system subjects women into untold miseries and the protagonists of Ambai survive them with mental courage and strong will. Married women in a patriarchal situation are sandwiched between the pressures exerted by their egoistic life partners and their personal likes and dislikes.

The story *A Kitchen in the Corner of a House (Veettin moolayil oru samaiyalarai)* focuses on the life of the downtrodden section of the society under patriarchal system. It discloses the pathetic plight of domestic women reeling under the pressure of household work in the limited space allotted to them in the house. Their sufferings, desires, and suggestions go unnoticed and unheeded by the men folk at home. The first part of the story describes in general the lifestyle of Rajasthanis. As the title indicates, the kitchen in the house, and the life of Rajasthanis centers around it. All the Rajasthanis both men and women, are fond of food and drinks. They eat a lot and enjoy different kinds of drinks. Sadly enough, the kitchen is not given sufficient space in a house. It is unhygienic, inadequately lit, and ventilated. Even to clean the vessels, there is no proper place.

The second part of the story is devoted to the world of women in the kitchen. Kitchen is the place completely allotted to women. No man enters it but commands for food. Inside the kitchen, where women reign, there seems to be a hierarchy. Padi Jeeji dominated it and Jeeji did odd jobs when his grandfather was alive. After his death Padi Jeeji has been given vegetarian food and is denied meat and drinks. But Padi Jeeji used to adopt tricks like being possessed with divine power and demanding drinks. "It was a food war. The protagonists are: Jiji, Bari-Jiji. When grandfather was alive, Bari-Jiji ruled absolutely and tyrannically. Jiji kneaded mountains of chapati dough. She sliced baskets of onions and kilos of meat. She roasted papads in the evening while Bari-Jiji drank her kesar kasturi. She made the pakoras. She fried entrails. Then grandfather died. Within ten days Jiji was sworn into power. Bari-Jiji lost her rights to kumkum, betel leaves, meat and spirits; she also lost in the matter of everyday meals. Every day there was meat cooked in the kitchen. In a democratic spirit, the vegetarians in the family (actually only Bari-Jiji) were served potatoes. Bari-Jiji celebrated her loss in the battlefield with loud belching all night long, by breaking wind as if her whole body was tearing apart, and then muttering in the toilet".

The author ironically says that ornaments do not beautify women but enslave her. Kitchen is like a prison where the women are foolishly happy taking decisions on food preparations.

The third part of the story is about the role of women in a family while undertaking a picnic. The whole family decides to go on a picnic to Sagar Lake wherein they can spot at that time of the year many beautiful birds. The author lists various things women have to do as preliminary arrangements for a one day picnic. Men never help them. Women alone struggle in the kitchen to prepare food for the whole lot and pack things and dresses necessary for children, men and themselves. While they sit in the kitchen throughout the night, men sleep peacefully and in the morning they get up late as usual only to say that women are happy doing all these things. Even in the picnic spot, women do not have time to sit and stare. The elderly women have to look after the needs of youngsters and men such as supplying food and water.

The last and the fourth part of the story form the climax wherein the author, through the character of Minakshi gives a solution to the problem of the oppressed woman. Jeeji suffers seriously from heart attack and is bed ridden. She worries about her kitchen authority more than her health or her family. She thinks about the work she has done in that kitchen for years together. She is reminded of the rich dresses and jewels she possesses. "My wedding skirt. It was bright red, with gold and silvere decorations all over. Twelve gold bangles. Two necklaces. Earstuds in pearls and red and green gemstones. Another set of earstuds in coral. Five sovereigns worth of centerpiece to the gold headband. A silver key-hook".

She explains to Minakshi how she had to continue her work in the kitchen immediately after abortion and at the death bed of the son in order to fulfill the needs of men folk at home. And Minakshi explains to her that her strength comes neither from her jewels nor from her dress, advises her to come out of all these things to which woman has attached her through ages to find out who she is. Suppose she had not done all this work in the family, she might have become a poet or a painter or a scientist or a peace-maker. She advises her to free herself from the stigma attached to her as a female. Jeeji too tries to do it, avoiding her fear, and clutches her hand to get support.

Thus Minakshi succeeds in redeeming her mother-in-law from the age-long mental suppression. The story presents women steeped in ignorance and false happiness in Indian society and men enjoying upper hand position and enslaving women for their happy lives. Women are treated by them as sexual objects to appease their sexual desires and servants to look after their other needs and to rear their children. The story vividly pictures how the slavish women in the kitchen get out of life with their spouses who live mainly to wine and dine. The story advises women to come out of the kitchen, to participate in the activities of the outside world, to lead independent lives and to shake off the traditional symbols imposed on them as women.

The next story *Kattill Oru Man (A Deer in the Forest)* focuses on the character of Thangam Aunty as narrated by a young girl. Thangam is an expert in telling stories of anti-traditional nature. Even the stories from the Ramayana and the Mahabharata would be narrated by her in an uncommon way- the wicked characters as good ones and vice versa. Some of her stories are without end, some without beginning and middle, some poetic and creating just images. Each and every one of the children like her stories. In her house she is seen everywhere. Though black complexioned, she is beautiful and good at music. Everyone is sympathetic towards her as she never comes of age. All measures such as medical treatment, poojas and mantras were taken but of no use. Her husband decides to marry second time, she attempts suicide but later she herself arranges for his second marriage.

Though the young narrator cannot understand fully what is wrong with their aunt, she understands that everything her aunt touches brings new life and vigour. Her aunt's body is full of life. Her touch brings relief to others especially during a woman's delivery. Though she never has that experience of being a mother, she feels happy with the children in the house.

One night the aunt tells the children a deer story. All animals in a forest are very happy. One day a deer loses its way while drinking water from a stream. It reaches a new forest and is quite scared of everything there but soon it gets used to all the places in it and feels at home. The children, on hearing the story, fall asleep while the aunt sits amidst them.

The story is allegorical in the sense that the deer alludes to Thangam. Her happy life in the old forest refers to her happy life before marriage. New forest refers to her married life. At first Thangam was like that deer lost itself in a new forest confused, unhappy and uncertain of things. Soon she finds happiness in her life. Thangam converting her own story into an animal fable shows her maturity and objective way of looking at life. Thangam is more imaginative and innovative than others. Children love her; she too loves and serves all, without having any grudge or grievance in her mind. This trait of hers elevates her to a high level though she does not attain womanhood and motherhood. She does not carry a taboo with her. Her inability to produce children does not mean that she is sterile. She can grow plants wonderfully and she can relieve other's pain quickly. Her life is no way incomplete. Thus the author breaks the myth surrounding a woman and insists that a happy life depends on one's attitude towards life.

The next story *Unpublished Manuscript (Prasurikkappatatha Kaippirathi)* is narrated by Senthamarai. Retrospection and introspection are the major tools used by Ambai. Senthamarai, in her teens, is highly imaginative and can think deeply. She is often in a reflective mood, imagining herself to be a great personality or a goddess. She likes to wander along the banks of river Ganga and knows every detail about it. She is also interested in writing traditional as well as modern verse. She listens to the songs sung by her mother. She loves her mother very much. Her mother always induces her to think in different ways. She used to tell her the lives of poets and other great personalities and all these make her a feminist, questioning the attitude of males represented in literature, films and biographies. Her house has been a meeting place for many poets and writers especially on Fridays. The discussions on poems, translations and sometimes striking poetic lines make a deep impression on her.

Though her mother lives separately from her husband, she never fails to analyze her husband Muthukumaran's poems and lectures. She never cares for others' criticism. Thirumagal tells her daughter, "It is easier for her to live with the poems of one like Muthukumaran than the man in him".

When she immerses herself deep in her work, she never minds taking food or doing household work. Senthamarai only compels her at times to take a little food. After the work is over, both the mother and the daughter together cook food with full involvement. The mother rejects proposals from her friends to remarry, just to maintain her relationship with her daughter. Thus the mother and the daughter live together in a peaceful and a happy comportment, influencing and shaping each other's mind and psyche.

Meanwhile, the daughter receives the 'unpublished manuscript' written by her mother. The daughter reads it many times; each reading reveals her mother's different persona. The manuscript gives on account of her mother's life, from her childhood till her separation from her husband. The manuscript begins with the grandfather Ramasamy leaving Malaysia after the death of his wife to settle in Madras, with the three year old daughter, Thirumagal, after the Second World War. He buys a printing press and starts a publishing company in Madras. His principle is to publish books in Tamil literature, folk songs, religious books, school books, and science books. He, never much pressurised, refuses to publish non-standard books, books on superstitions, and even notices encouraging rituals. He has his own views on widow remarriage. His opinion is that widows should remarry not to be under the protection of a man, as that view reflects as though men sacrifice themselves by giving life to a widow. Ramasamy himself marries a widow in Malaysia and allows her to study as much as she likes in madras. He never permits anyone to praise him saying that he has given life to a widow as that very word widow will hurt her. Ramasamy respects his wife and loves her. The letters exchanged by them are proof of the deep love that existed between them. Ramasamy is good at cooking and interested in listening to music, loves his daughter very much, and allows her to do her higher studies. He never engages her in doing household work. Sometimes he gets the assistance of his daughter in the works interrelated to the press.

When his daughter, Thirumagal decides to marry Muthukumaran, a poet, he agrees. But Muthukumaran proves to be a male chauvinist, a drunkard, a drug addict and one who values his friends more than his wife. When she is pregnant, there breaks out a quarrel between them. Muthukumaran wants her to be a wife doing household works, serving him and his friends. Thirumagal refuses to be one such wife. Muthukumaran goes to the extent of beating her. Senthamarai is born and Ramasamy dies. The proprietorship of the press comes to her. Once she refuses to publish Muthukumaran's poems which bear a streak of violence against women, without consulting the publisher's board. Enraged, Muthukumaran beats her; she too beats him back. She is admitted to a mental asylum, brought back by her father's friends and then she decides to leave him. She sells the press, resigns her as a lecturer in Chennai and leaves for Benares on the day of the funeral ceremony of Annadurai, the former Chief Minister of Tamilnadu.

Senthamarai reads this manuscript several times; and wants to see her father's photo. She has also received an invitation to participate in the function by the Muthukumaran memorial committee on the occasion of the death anniversary of Muthukumaran. In a mechanical voice, the mother informs her about the death of Muthukumaran in a government hospital. Understanding her desire to see her father's photo, the mother shows her a framed photo in which her father is holding her. Senthamarai decides to attend the function. The mother does not object to it. Thirumagal could understand her daughter's desire to see her father, as she experiences deep affection for her father. Thirumagal in the story was brought up in an ambience of atheism propagated by her rationalist father. Senthamarai says that, "never seen her mother performing puja or going to the temple".

The story explores the figure of a mother emerging as a symbol of sacrifice, an epitome of intelligence, and high understanding. She loves her husband's poems, though she hates him as a person. Indirectly the author seems to say how an educated woman has to face life is explained. Love, humour, and pathos are found mixed together. The story begins and ends with a reference to a commemorative function in honour of Muthukumaran. Senthamarai decides to attend it as she says, "can receive his collection of poems in their proper spirit".

The next story *Parasakthi etc. in Plastic Box (Plastic Tappavil Parasakthi Muthaliyor)* is about a traditional Indian mother who explains and glorifies the concept of motherhood. The mother is not just an individual but an institution. The mother of two daughters Thanam and Bharathi and a son, Thinakaran, she creates her own world. Though steeped in Indian culture and tradition, she can make her own circle wherever she goes. Her only watchword is love- love for all human beings and all animals. With her love, she encompasses everyone and at the same time she stands out like a tower among all. Her love transcends her family and encircles the whole world. She is independent and fights for rights and justice.

The mother feeds crows every morning without fail wherever she is. She is interested in cooking different kinds of dishes, preparing medicines for family use, gardening, embroidery, politics and singing. When her elder daughter Bharathi who lives in America, becomes a divorcee, she goes to America to console her. There, the mother moves freely with the people in the airport, and later with the neighbours of Bharathi. Without feeling tired, she prepares dishes and medicines necessary for the people around her. Since she cannot find crows in America, she starts feeding large squirrels. She always carries a plastic box which contains images of all Indian Gods. She is highly religious and creates a place for her plastic box. She regularly worships and offers pooja to all her gods. She never asks her daughter about her divorce or her husband Kumarasamy. But without the knowledge of her daughter, she visits Kumarasamy's house and gets back all the jewels and vessels belonging to Bharathi.

After the death of the father, the mother has to vacate her rental house. Thanam, the younger daughter, urges her to come to her house, though she is not well-off. The mother agrees but finds it difficult to choose the necessary things and discard the unnecessary ones, from among the various vessels and things collected and stored by her since her marriage. Hence she keeps all those articles in a safe place, chooses only a few among which are her Veena and plastic box and takes them to Thanam's house. There too the mother as usual is busy engaging herself in many activities. But she seems to be sad, as she desires to be in her house, she also longs to have her own garden and to write her autobiography and does not reveal all her desires to Thanam but Thanam understands her mother's feelings and decides to buy the same rental house.

The story upholds motherhood and celebrates the relationship between mother and daughters and exemplifies the relationship between sisters. It breaks down tradition- tradition of mother living with her son after the death of her husband, the tradition of mother being dependent on husband and son, and the traditional outlook on mother as a woman who knows nothing about the external world and has little knowledge about world affairs.

In the story *Sirakukal Muriyum*, Saya, mother of a child and married for ten years endures the loveless, emotionless and unhappy life with Baskaren. Her domestic life becomes hard as her husband neither appreciates her work nor cares for her feelings. Her sexual life is uninteresting and dull. Saya struggles to contain herself as her husband, an officer of no mean income, is too obsessed with money to allow her to fulfill even her small desires. Her relationship with her neighbours and relatives break because of her husband's stingy and miserly bent of mind and she feels depressed. When her sister-in-law enquiries her: "you are not at all interested in anything. Why are you, then?" She replies "to live and only to live. What else can be the reason?".

When she conceives her second child after a long gap, she does not feel happy as her husband immediately calculates the child as an additional expense of money. She feels "like a bird lost its wings" but "she confines herself deplorably to bed, subdued by her zealous force to get rid of it".

Her decision to live with her husband is probably born out of her concern for her son and yet-to-be-born child. She lacks will and courage to face her problems, yet she survives.

The marriage of Saya and Baskaran, is beneath the surface, a living hell or a cosmic disaster. The dominant theme is the apathy of the male spouse and the disillusionment of the woman. In college friends used to call her a beautiful dreamer. But, "all those pearls which had been stored in her mind had been turned into so many stones".

Her awfully obese and miserly man in memorable drawn as one who is always counting the cost of the things that they really need to be happy in life. Her desperate efforts to reduce her dependence on him for money through her decision to be a paid dressmaker show how she considers it, "a kind of stupidity to try and change him and to oppose him in a vain battle".

It is in her most miserable moments that she formulates in her mind a series of laws to prevent female frustrations and male apathy.

1. There should be a law preventing men from "bloating out" into potbellies.

2. The next law says that men who have "hairless, slippery chests should never marry".

3. Another law forbids those men to kiss who chew too many betel leaves and make their teeth look "like pieces of crushed tin".

4. The fourth law provides for confiscation of the purse "if a husband tightened his fingers upon his purse the minute his wife looked at an object with desire".

5. A Draconian law framed by her says "men who have no kind feelings should be made to have vasectomies and forcibly prevented from having children".

6. As Munrovian and Ambaian heroines regard "sex as a wholesome... indulgence, like dancing and night dinners" there is a law stipulating that women who have "not read the Kama Sutra should not be allowed to marry

7. A husband who makes advances when he is not wanted should be given a house "in the red light district in perpetuity".

8. Legal proceedings should be taken against Tamil films which portray women as renouncers.

9. She is so anguished in the end at wedlock's demand of her most cherished dreams as a sacrifice that she no longer bothers to think of the last law "... to remove all the obstructions in the way of a woman's independence"

The abstract, homogenized women figure, as inscribed and promoted by the nationalist patriarchal/paternalistic discourse is punctured by the two writers' de-idealized, realistic portrayal of women. All the above protagonists suffer dehumanization. Mahasweta Devi and Ambai debunk mythicized deification of the characters by exposing its circumscribing/delimiting potential that contains women within their historically prescribed roles and thus denies them their individuality. Despite their age, the women struggle a lot to keep themselves alive. Flora Alexander rightly states that the creative energies of contemporary women novelists produce work that explores vast tracts of human experience and is marked by a rich diversity of approach. Thus Mahasweta Devi and Ambai's fiction expresses diverse experiences of middle class Indian women and multiple dimensions of their lives. And the stories prove that female experiences are valuable and precious and form an integral part of human experiences in entirety. The writers seem to suggest that sacrifice on the part of the victims of oppression is not only inevitable to defend their inalienable rights as members of the human family, but, it is the mark of the ultimate victory of the human values and an unmistakable pointer to the defeat of the inhumanity of the oppressor.

The two writers invest their female narrators with the power to annotate their stories in such a way as to transcend differences of gender. The creative impulse for both the authors comes from renewed contact with the lost mother but the phallic presence is eagerly sought for creativity in the post- feminist phase which demands new discourses and new ways of thinking. Mahasweta Devi and Ambai have produced their best stories which highlight the crisis in man- woman relationship. The significantly separate sections of their stories are all parts of their individual visions of life. The different sections are inseparable parts of a portrait presenting life in all its variety.

Amidst the never ending class struggle that the writers have so effectively portrayed, the struggle of gender becomes the issue of highlight. In poverty and prosperity the two writers remain identical. In the search for the self, they try to discover a language through which the subaltern may speak. 'Tears' that have been eternally associated with the female become the unique language of the feminine to speak for themselves in Devi and Ambai. The writers draw a tender and sensitive picture of women caught in the socio-political system of oppression within which they are forced to survive. Injustice and poverty can be overcome only through socio-political balancing of will-power for the betterment of human life combined with a touch of understanding and humanism. The writers leave the narrative open to possibilities and refuse to prescribe rigid contextualization of the individual characters within the larger socio-political economic historical critique.

Mahasweta Devi and Ambai's stories are a study in human nature, of the simple joys and sorrows of the life of the downtrodden, the exploitation and sufferings and conditions of abject poverty in which they live their lives. Joseph Warrant Beach in his book, *The Twentieth Century Novel* points out that: ... Philosophical novelists are often extremely able story-tellers. But it is evident that it is not to the story that they attach most importance, but to the social, economic, and political lessons which are to be derived from it.

IV
LANGUAGE AND STYLE

This chapter exhibits the usage of language and style of Mahasweta Devi and Ambai. It elicits the imagery, mystery, similes employed in the novel, and also focuses on the poetic style of the authors.

Style masks and reveals the true, primal soul of the writer, who is struggling toward self realization. The vocation of fiction is vigilant insistence of the writer on making his or her developing style a continued transformation of the hidden into the revealed. Style is not simply a matter of literary, verbal habit but part of the whole sense of a man himself as a member of society and perhaps as a shaper of the society to which he belongs.

It affirms the style of language writers in focus and tries to correlate their content and form. The writers' writing career spans over a period of five decades, and their form is bound to have been transitional and should have evolved with them in nature. The narrative technique is not simple; it uses elements of satire, myth, history to construct a strong appeal to the social conscience of readers. It illuminates the frustrations, conflicts and contradictions faced by the women protagonists. They use language as the primary driving source that guides their appreciation of the intrinsic worth of human beings. They make use of every available opportunity to pronounce their vision and voice for the voiced less people.

The translated works of the authors from source text to target language is not always smooth, since the narratives are especially difficult to translate. The translations of the works remain valuable as a means of accessing the writings of one of the major Indian writers of our time. The stories are in a distinctive style, pose particular challenges for the translator, because of the rich linguistic layering of the original texts.

The narrative of Ambai is totally different from the traditional way of narrative. The traditional narrative has an organized structure of a monolithic plot with sequence of events in time and facts, is linear, singular, logical and progressive. The narrative techniques of Mahasweta Devi and Ambai are more experimental than argumentative; their movement is more fluid than direct. They use multiple devices to communicate her polyphonic experience.

The multiple mechanisms employed by Ambai can be broadly divided into three: Form, Techniques and Literary devices. The Form refers to the structure and progression of events in a literary work. Each traditional work has a defined form: a beginning, middle and an end. Ambai's fiction disrupts the traditional form and pattern, and innovates unique forms. Commenting on the various forms experimented by Ambai in her fiction, Lakshmi Holmstrom writes that her stories are intricate and layered, moving between different narrative voices and ties. Ambai's stories have anti- linear plots with modified forms that constitute a polyphonic narrative typical of the postmodern era.

Veetin Moolaiyil Oru Samayalarai (A Kitchen in the Corner) consists of a series of four scenes in a Rajasthani joint family during the summer holidays. The first two scenes establish the centrality of Kitchen, the lives of women and define their power politics and roles; the third is a picnic by the side of a lake, wherein ironically the women picnickers indulge in food preparation. The last scene describes Jiji, the mother-in-law at her deathbed with the suggestions of her freedom of the self from the world of kitchen.

Atavi in twelve parts parallels the isolated life and search for peace of the modern woman Senthiru in the forest with that of Sita, the heroine of the Indian epic *The Ramayana*. The odd numbered parts of the story deal with the forest life of Senthiru in stream-of-consciousness narrative consummating in Senthiru attaining peace of mind from the philosophic utterances of sixty year old sanyasi cum musician. The even numbered divisions are Senthiru's reconstructed story of Sita- starting from Sita writing her Sitaayanam deconstructing the image of divine husband ending in Sita's acceptance of Ravana's friendship but desiring to lead an independent life. Lakshmi Holmstrom writes in her introduction to Ambai about such creative attempts at novel forms: "there is a kind of exhilaration in this playing with forms at the height of her work, in what looks like postmodernist techniques of multiple perspectives- many voices, fragmented and interspersed narratives- techniques which are normally used in the postmodern novel rather than in the short story". Such mixing of various forms in the fiction of Ambai has created enough room for her to narrate her female experiences.

Technique means the way the story is presented and the stream-of-consciousness narrative or the interior monologue exposes the frustration and repression experienced by her energetic and determined female protagonists, as of their sex.

Sirakukal Muriyum depends largely on the interior monologues of Saya, whose thoughts ruminate over her urge to disobey her patriarchal husband's words. *Atavi* exposes Senthiru's psychological struggle in achieving peace of mind.

Flashback technique, a part of stream-of- consciousness narrative, is used to present a flash-view of the past events. It enables the author to check or break the linearity and to achieve cyclical time sequence and thereby introducing anti-traditional ways of handling the technique. Ambai analyses the past lives of her protagonists and their mothers as a continuation of their present miseries. They vary in each story in their length, mode and significance.

Saya in *Sirakukal Muriyum* introspects over her life at both natal and marital houses. Her memory activates her understanding that her adjustments and adaptations with her obese, obstinate and stingy husband do not bring in any change in his character; instead she is subjected to psychological changes. She finds a companion- sufferer in her mother while she looks deep into her mother's life with her possessive husband.

The flashback technique is differently employed in *Pirasurikkapatatha Kaippirathi.* Thirumagal writes about her past life in manuscript form titled 'Tiruvasakam'-'Tiru' being the short epithet by which she is called by her intimate friends and relatives. Vasakam means writing. This manuscript remains unpublished as it is specially meant for her only daughter Senthamarai and it narrates how Thirumagal, a divorcee now, was treated brutally by her husband, Muthukuaran. On reading the manuscript, Senthamarai comes to know about father and also about the sufferings of her mother. She reads many times on different occasions and each reading gives different interpretations. Her successive readings of the manuscript enable her to come to proper terms with her parents- she could sympathize with her mother for her sufferings; at the same time she could not detest her father on recognition of his being a great poet. This long flashback not emanated directly from the consciousness of the person who experienced the events but narrated by the daughter renders a unique objectivity to the whole story.

In *Atavi*, Ambai manipulates the flashback technique in a still more complex and intricate manner. Senthiru staying in a forest recalls her past life in Bombay. Her memory delves deep into her birth, the circumstances which led to her separation from her family after many years of happy married life. In the forest, with a vow to rewrite epics, Senthiru begins to rewrite the Ramayana from Sita's point of view and names it *Sitaayanam*. The select episodes in the life of Sita are revised in third person narrative: her birth, her marriage with Rama, her life in the forest, the war waged by Rama to restore her to Ayoti and Rama's suspiciousness about her chastity- all these incidents run parallel to Senthiru's life experiences. This flashback within flashback technique- one by Sita, an ancient mythic heroine and another by Senthiru, a modern woman-reveals the unchanging plight of women through ages and their sufferings in a male dominated Indian society. Most of Ambai's flashbacks either reason out the present plight of the protagonist or enable her decision in her life. Except in *Atavi*, they erupt and explode when the emotional protagonist is at the verge of tolerance.

Dreams and fantasies are devices used in a stream-of-consciousness narrative to emphasize the inner lives of the characters which are markedly different from the roles they play. They also focus on the gulf between inner and outer selves of the characters. Dreams happen in the present and often express unfulfilled wishes or the confusion in the mind. They take place unconsciously while the character is sleeping or in a relaxed mood. Fantasies are daydreams about the future and they occur voluntarily and consciously.

Dreams abound in Ambai's stories and they project the troubled psyche of an Indian middle class woman. Senthiru's dream in *Atavi* takes her back to the days at her natal home. In her dream, she runs fast as if somebody chased her. After a long run through the path full of pits, she reaches the railway station. She breathes hard while getting into a railway compartment; the train reaches another station where she sees her father sitting on a bench on the platform. When her father asks her to get down as he is waiting only for her, she replies she cannot as she has luggage. The train moves, while both of them stretch their hands towards each other from their places. The train probably stands for her life, and her worries or heaviness in her heart, the dream continues, even after the train moves.

In a half-awaken stage, Senthiru sees the image of her blind music teacher and then her own father staggers like the music teacher. This merging of two figures- her music teacher and her father- can be correlated with a sanyasi who teaches Senthiru the secret of happiness later at the end of the narrative.

Flashbacks, dreams and fantasies in a stream-of-consciousness narrative flash the inner life of women. The plots of Ambai's stories are thin and the characters are limited as is characteristic of stream-of-consciousness narrative. All the stories, whether they are in first person point of view or third person point of view, narrate women's perspectives and experiences. Neither structure of the plot is restrained by any argumentation nor is it determined by any rules of composition. Hence the stories do not have a beginning, middle and an end as well as their movement is anti-linear and anti-traditional.

Literary devices such as imagery, symbol, allusions, irony and descriptions enable the authors to reveal their experiences in a creative manner. Imagery, in its literary work or a unit of a literary sense, means the collection of images within a literary work. These image clusters are sometimes pointers to the unconscious motivations of the author. Ambai has made wide use of imagery in her works.

Ambai's imagery can be categorized under three headings: nature, mirror and colour. Ambai's imagery drawn from nature associates her female protagonists with fundamental life in nature. Birds with their power of flight are traditional emblems of freedom and human spirit. In Ambai's *Veettin Moolaiyil Oru Samaiyalarai*, bird imagery signals the aspiration and freedom of women in a society. Picnicking near Sagar Lake, the Rajasthani women are circumscribed to look after the biological needs of their men and children. They have no time to watch the migratory water birds with red beaks flying beautifully over and above the surface of water. Those water birds are free but not these women. Kusuma, one of the daughters-in-law over the recent loss of her pregnancy, equates the unformed fetus with those beautiful small birds.

Mahasweta Devi in her story *The Five Women* describes nature as, "A Pearl, silly, a pearl. First it's born inside an oyster, in the water. Then it's taken out when the oyster is pried open, this time on land". In another description she says' "Of course! The women, the men, the old people! Why do you think I was named Godhumi? My skin was the colour of the ripe wheat, so my grandmother said, let's call her Godhumi ... All day long the boys and girls shout, make a noise, keep the birds at bay. We make huge scarecrows of straw to frighten off the birds".

Forest imagery in *Atavi* purports to deconstruct the patriarchy prejudiced view that forest is a place of punishment for women and all creations in the forest- for instance, trees, flowers and deer – mislead women who require the help of a man to rescue her from such dangers. Senthiru, the heroine of the story, challenges such views when she says, " it is time to rewrite the epic" , thereby blasting the myth that forest is not suitable for good solitary women and only enticers like Menaka can go alone into the forest. Senthiru lives in the forest alone and by sharing silent moments with the objects in the forest, tries to attain peace of mind. There she rewrites the story of Sita, Who too lived alone in the forest.

Mirror motif occurs in Ambai's *Pirasurikkappatatha kaippirathi.* The narrator Senthamarai in her narrative remembers an egg-shaped and -framed mirror in the inner room of her house. Standing before the mirror, she, as a school girl, used to assume various roles of the celebrities in India such as Bharathi and ouvai without any gender distinctions. She will cast different looks- a ferocious look at an imaginary unjust man and a calm solemn look to attract others. She tries to be a desexualized personality using her creative brain and at the same time reflects her moral awareness and social values.

Besides imagery, a rich fund of symbols is extensively used by Ambai. Generally, a symbol evokes an object that suggests the meaning. In *Veettin Moolaiyil Oru Samayalarai,* the kitchen denotes the limited space for women in the family. The only window in the kitchen which lets in neither air nor light suggests confinement. 'Wings' in *Sirakukal Muriyum,* symbolizes freedom-freedom for Saya from the clutches of her non- understanding husband.

Ruthraveena in *Atavi* is a symbol of female life. Sita asserts Ravana who is about to help her in lifting ruthraveena. "it is my life; many people have played with my life like a ball; atleast hereafter let me take it with my own hands". This symbolism is explicitly drawn, denoting that women can be and should be the gynocracy of their own lives.

The story *The Five women* of Mahasweta Devi is with hands full of similes. She says, "Like a lotus in full Moon she was". And in *Kunti and the Nishadins* when karma is dead Kunti utters, "Gandhari's piercing cry at the sight of Karnas body struck me like a whip" , Jashoda in Mahasweta Devi's *Breast Stories* states' "When Kangali's body didn't drill her body like a geologist in a darkness lit only by an oil". And in the same story Mahasweta Devi conveys Jashoda's misfortune as, "A Female's life hangs on like a turtle's - her heart breaks but no word is uttered - the woman will burn, her ashes will fly/praise on high".

Ambai uses satire to probe into the defects in the world. Satire is used to expose humanities vices and foibles giving impetus to change or reform through ridicule. In *Veettin Moolayil Oru Samaiyalarai*, Ambai satirizes the power politics of women inside the kitchen. While women are being oppressed by men, women out of ignorance enjoy their subordinate position. Kitchen is like an incarceration center to them but they mistake it to be their 'queendom' and take decisions on the menu. Ambai calls it 'cowardly authority' and satirises their decisions as big decisions. Ambai wants such women to come out of their shells to have awareness of their own selves and their rights.

In Ambai's *Veettin Moolaiyil Oru Samayalarai*, Meenatchi, the daughter-in-law, descriptively recalls the astonishing amount of work done by her mother-in-law, Jiji. "once every four weeks, the wick of the store has to be cleaned and pulled up; whenever kerosene is available, it has to be bought and stored; in the rainy season the rice and the dhal have to be watched for pests; in the mango season, pickles have to be prepared; in the summer, pappada; in the fruit season, sherbet, juice jam; old clothes to be discarded; kitchen to be washed once in two weeks".

Ambai celebrates the body of an old woman in *Veettin Moolayil Oru Samaiyalarai*. The old woman Jiji's body is compared to a 'fully ripe fruit with its skin shrunken'. The nerves and the scars on her body are not only the marks of old age but also the marks left by her body as a female- the marks left after the delivery of children in her lower abdomen and the dark lines created by the jewels worn around her neck. It is the 'lived body' as it has done its duties to perpetuate the human race. The description glorifies the old female body.

How a woman looks at a man is described in *Pirasurikkappatatha Kaippirathi.* Thirumagal, the protagonist of the story, describes her lover's physical appearance and his dress. She describes his black, ugly crackly feet with untrimmed nails on his fingers as that which unite him with the earth.

The intensity that constitutes Mahasweta Devi's thematic is further buttressed in its agenda of resistance by an equally potent aesthetic intervention that virtually ruptures the classical 'art for art's sake' form-active paradigm. The present chapter attempts to understand and evaluate various facets of Mahasweta Devi and Ambai's resistant aesthetic enterprise as it impinges on the structure, narration, language, and other allied features of their works. Their resistant aesthetics manifest itself in their deconstructive-subalterns' narrative strategies of subversion and inversion, expansion and modification that primarily appear in her narratives as:

1. Fudging of the boundaries between the literary and the non-literary;

2. Subversion and inversion of the conventional literary symbols, Stereotypes, myths;

3. Expansion of the contours of the activist narratives by dislocating its conventional binary paradigms, investing the endings of her narratives with gaps and ambivalences, and appropriating the tools of narration to reorient the response of her target readers;

4. De-tabooing and de-gendering of the stereotypical symbols, myths and imagery, rupturing of the conventional linguistic canon and moulding of language into an enabling, empowering tool, destabilizing the 'standard' structures of linguistic usage with the ironically-inverted semantics of their narratives.

Mahasweta Devi's literary oeuvre is poised on the aesthetic tripod of creation, critique, and conditioning. This three-fold narrative agenda entails an unavoidable intervention into the conventional canonicity through the strategies of confrontation, expansion, inversion, and renovation.

Mahasweta's fictional art is an amalgam of journalistic endeavour, activist intervention and literary creation. These three facets of her creativity manifest themselves in numerous blends in her literature. As Gayatri Chakravorty Spivak notes, "her writing and her activism reflect one another, they are precisely that – 'a folding back upon one another – reflection in the root sense ... Indeed, if one reads carefully, one may be seen as the other's difference".

Her fiction not only highlights the exploitation but also actively participates in the subaltern's struggle against and attacks the exploitative system and the forces perpetrating it not only by exposing these in her fictional narratives but also by explicitly accusing them by way of the authorial interventions that run parallel to the fabula.

Mahasweta's stories are invariably organized along this triple-axis of her personality. *Behind the Bodice: Choli Ke Pichhe*, for example, opens with an extended journalistic piece where the author sheds the inhibition of conventional storytelling and makes a sweeping survey of the contemporary issues of 'national' importance thus: What is there, was the national problem that year. When it became a national issue, the other fuckups of that time- e.g. crop failure- earthquake, everywhere clashes between so called terrorists and state power and therefore killings, the beheading of a young man and woman in Haryana... , hundreds of rape murder, lockup torture et cetera non-issues ... all this remained non-issues. Much more important than this was *choli ke pichche – behind the bodice.*

The narrative takes off in the manner of a satirical newspaper comment on contemporary socio-political development lending it a highly topical character. Everyone got busy to find out what was there: national media, censor-board, liberated anti-bra girls–many associations-organisations ... cable-tv channels – green eyeshaded lady votarians' associations – all the religious groups – and politicians. Watching cassettes of Khalnayak undercover became the 'norm of the day' ... India suddenly discovered that behind the bodice was the Middle East ... That powerful lobby which is engaged in sending messages to the brain of the youthful generation to the effect that Bombay films are the cultural medium for representing Indian popular culture, that lobby was pissed off at this.

Such a mumble-jumble of news items reflects the superficial amorphousness of the contemporary media-ted reality. In her characteristic ironically-humorous tone, Mahasweta pens a powerful critique of the modern 'nation', its "Bombay films"/Bollywood-inspired plastic culture that passes off as popular culture, along with the front-runners of the 'nation', viz., the national media, various social organization, religious and political groups, and politicians. Even the elite intellectual does not escape Mahasweta's critical vision. Her incisive wit pierces through the cultural façade to expose its intellectual bankruptcy and foreground it's sensationalism: The word 'invasion' worries the nation ... Now from the entire country, Indian intellectuals not knowing a single Indian language meet in a closed seminar in the capital city and make the following wise decision known. Cultural invasion is much more dangerous than cultural revolution. So India is doing what India must do to hold it back ... The natural vacuum must be filled with pirated cassettes. In that sense *Behind the Bodice or Choli Ke Pichche* is an elixir for the times.

Through this journalistic foray, Mahasweta not only contextualises and contemporaries the setting but also conditions the reader as to the general drift of the story. First the title itself (taken as it is from the first line of a popular Hindi film song), and then the above quoted journalistic appendage that explicates upon the lyric, startles the reader with its sweeping analysis of contemporary contexts. The parodic dig turns into scathing irony exposing the commercial exploitation hidden 'behind the bodice' of the subaltern Gangor that ultimately leads to a tragic but prophetic climax of the fictional narrative.

The narrative features Mahasweta's fictional oeuvre – with the help of which she interrogates the conventional canonicity –in her strategies of subversion and inversion of the conventional stereotypes, symbols and myths. These strategies not only enable her to interrogate the contemporary from the point of view of the subaltern but also help her to forge a literary style that deconstructs as it creates. This facet of her literary praxis is the most pronounced in her treatment of myths and received stereotypes as these impinge on the lives of the subalterns.

Myth as a classical, predetermined, prehistoric given discourse has been questioned and qualified by Mahasweta in many of her fictional narratives. Mahasweta employs the critical trope of irony to dislocate/invert the mythical which serves as the discursive exposition of the given knowledge. While exposing contemporary hierarchical hegemonic structures, Mahasweta invokes the mythical to expose the hegemonies written within such narratives. A consistent problematising, expanding and revising of myth characterises the poetics of her resistant writing. She explores the sites, modes and extent of resistance within the economies of myth.

In her fictional narratives, she indirectly attacks the dominant mythical narratives as these control and condition the class-caste and gendered relations in Indian society. From the narrative position of a distant observer, she satirically exposes the ironies wrought upon the subaltern lives by the mythical master-narratives. In *Breast Giver* Mahasweta ruptures the construct of motherhood that serves to circumscribe the female agency by busting the myth of the Holy Suckling Mother, Yashoda. The Haldar Mistress, impressed as she is by Jashoda's massive 'mammal projections' calls her the 'legendary Cow of Fulfilment'. Not only the upper class, privileged female but her de-classed, deprivileged husband also participates in perpetrating the politics of mythical interpolation on the life of the gendered subaltern. Kangali is enlightened by the spirit of 'Brahma the Creator' as he appeals to the discursive sanctities internalised by his wife: 'You'll have milk in your breast only if you have a child in your belly ... You are a faithful wife, a goddess. You will yourself be pregnant, be filled with a child, rear it at your breast, isn't this why Mother came to you as a midwife?'.

The sublimation of the maternal role is directed towards the containment of women by promise of greater glory. This deification offered to her is a kind of 'mythical bind' – a device to control the female and her agency.

Mahasweta inverts the mythical idea of motherhood by presenting her protagonist as a 'professional mother' very much to the tune of the times as the world today belongs to the professional. The mythical Yashoda is completely demystified in the image of cancer ridden breasts of Jashoda that busted, putrefied and turned into volcanic craters. Mahasweta's concluding judgement strikes the final de (con) structure blow to the pieties of 'motherhood'; "Jashoda was God manifest; others do and did whatever she thought. Jashoda's death was also the death of God. When a mortal masquerades as God here below, she is forsaken by all and she must always die alone".

Draupadi, of Mahasweta's *Breast Stories* draws on the tale of Mahabharata evincing ironic parallels with the epic. The narrative is strategically positioned as a violent subversion of the significations of the mythic tale. Mahasweta reveals her modus operandi thus: "It is essential to revive existing myths and adopt them to the present times and following the oral tradition, create new ones as well. While I find the existing mythologies, epics and 'puranas' interesting, I use them with a new interpretation" .

Mahasweta revives the myth of *Draupadi* to expose its inherent semiotics of subjugation. Mahasweta's "Draupadi" is a story not of the 'rajvadhu' (the daughter-in-law of the emperor) Draupadi, but of the tribal aboriginal, Dopdi. In her refiguring of Draupadi, Mahasweta displaces her out of the 'sacrosanct' space, as well as out of class. She wrenches her out of the mythical to insert her into history. Mahasweta's Dopdi is a tribal woman engaged in the Naxalite insurgency of the late sixties. Dopdi is further displaced out of the patriarchal social institution of marriage. While Draupadi had five husbands to rule her and share her under a pact of partnership sealed and sanctioned by their mother, tribal Dopdi has had one husband who has already been killed when the narrative opens. Draupadi, a comrade associated with the naxalite movement, is now a fugitive on the run from the police. Mahasweta displaces and re-figures Draupadi, using her as a trope to etch her character anew with subversive overtones. Transformed as she is from the mythological Draupadi, Mahasweta's tribal Dopdi is the agent of a potential unmaking of gender and class containment. As in the case of Draupadi, Dopdi Mejhen is also victimised by the patriarchal order/state for being a woman and a revolutionary insurgent. This patriarchal hegemony and control is the only thing that has continued unchanged from mythical narratives through history to the present times. Everything else in their contexts has undergone transformation.

Draupadi is a woman of aristocratic lineage who shares and conforms in her conduct to the patriarchal ideological imperatives. When dishonoured and humiliated before the 'rajya sabha' (the court/assembly of the king), she appeals to the masculinity of those present to come to her rescue. When the 'respectable', 'mighty' males of her clan failed to save her honour, she turned to the beginning paternalism embodied by Krishna for help. The much-proclaimed rebellion of Draupadi remains constrained within the neat boundaries of the patriarchal system throughout the episode. Under the Godfather-ship and guardian-ship of the grand patriarch Krishna, her resistance and protest gets 'channelized' through the finely disciplined ideological constraints internalised by her as a woman.

In her re-figuration of Draupadi, Mahasweta not only localises her name (Draupadi is de-sanskritised and vernacularized to Dopdi) but indigenizes her habitat also. Her Dopdi is a woman of forests, an offspring of nature and so love for freedom and disregard and detestation of the attempts to control and curtail is a part of her basic instincts. Senanayak, a representative of modern patriarchal world-order in the story, while supporting Dopdi and her cause in theory, attempts a total decimation of the resisting "object" in practice. After capturing Dopdi with his strategic manoeuvring, Senanayak orders her "making." Dopdi's abuse doesn't stop short at the dignified, refined limits of an attempted 'vastraharan' (an act of forced disrobing) of the epic variety, it entails an absolute "making" of her exercised over 'a billion moons', 'a million light years'.

The tale of Dopdi out-performs that of the epic in terms of the ravages caused as well as the reaction displayed by the victim. Unlike her mythological namesake, Dopdi doesn't seek any divine intervention. The place of Dopdi's defiance is not the court of a 'Maharaja', it is the wild space of a forest. Dopdi gets no divine male rescuer The custodians of law offer her a piece of cloth to hide her shame after subjecting her to multiple-rape throughout the night. Dopdi pours down the water, tears the cloth to pieces and refuses to cover herself up with the male-defined notions of 'shame' and 'female modesty'. Covering herself up would have been a reaffirming and a fortification of the man-made morality preserved and sanctified by the patriarchal ideological constructs of 'female honour' and 'breach of woman's modesty (and her subjecthood?).'

However, the effectiveness of Dopdi's resistance is not the refusal to act, but the refusal to act predictably. She redefines the construct of "sexual honour" of a woman when she comes out naked and confronts Senanayak. Unlike the mythological Draupadi, she resists guilt, fear, shame or servility that are typically associated with the discourse of rape. Refusing to bow down to her "making" (in shame and servility), Dopdi challenges the brutalizer to "kounter" her and instead of lamenting at the loss of the supposed "respectability", she goes forward to question the masculinity of her maker. Dopdi's action totally dislocates and belittles the disciplined 'resistance' displayed by Draupadi's lamentations as she attempts to awaken the masculine powers of the great patriarchs in the grand epical narrative.

These inversions and subversions as narrative props in Mahasweta Devi lead to a literary praxis that instead of simplifying the issues at hand, pitchforks them into the complexity of the lived. It helps Mahasweta Devi transcend the pitfalls of the propagandist literature that is not only simplistic but is also locked within binary thinking. Mahasweta is able to successfully overcome the trap of simplistic binary narratives that becomes apparent the moment one focuses on the endings of her stories. One common accusation against the 'art for life's sake' kind of literature is that with its overt ideological thrust, it turns into propagandist literature which in its attempt to validate its governing ideology, tends to simplify the complexities of life. Such accusations should not lead one to construe that all politically oriented/active literature is propagandist. Mahasweta's interventionist literature, for example, resists such ideology driven over-simplification of solutions by enunciating a credo that is complexly nuanced and rooted in the reality of life. Such a literary credo is an integral part of her story-telling and can be vouched here from the way she ends her stories.

The endings of Mahasweta's stories steer clear of presenting simple, straightforward solutions. In her narratives, the solutions are premised upon complex, contradictory possibilities. *Draupadi,* for example, one of the most powerful of her protagonists, confronts Senanayak, denigrates his false masculinist pride and challenges him to 'kounter' her . Mahasweta concludes the story with Senanayak being 'afraid to stand before an unarmed target, terribly afraid' , getting pushed by the 'two mangled breasts' of Dopdi. Such a conclusion, however, cannot be interpreted as a resolution of Dopdi's situation. While Dopdi's reaction does dislocate the stability of state /gender/caste hegemonies, it can't be taken as 'the final' closure signifying the ultimate triumph of the subaltern over such hegemony and the impossibility of any further action. Senanayak, while being momentarily afraid of the unpredictable behaviour of Dopdi, is still the 'nayak' – the leader of the army of a sovereign, secular, patriarchal state. The story ends but the tremendous powers of the hegemonies of nation/gender/ class as embodied in Senanayak linger on and evince the possibility of retribution and appropriation of resistance.

In keeping with her deeply nuanced ideology driven literary agenda, Mahasweta builds her narratives along three narrative locations – the first of which is born out of popular consciousness and is rooted in experiential level, it is the location to which the subaltern belongs; the second is feudalistic/ modern and is born out of rationalism, this is the location of the dominant/the ruling/the haves who appropriate the subaltern; the third is the location of the author which brings the overriding authorial vision to the narrative. The juxtaposition and criss-crossing of the first two and the omni-presence of the third allows the author the scope to present a powerful critique of the class-caste, the political, religious and economic hierarchies.

Mahasweta's narrative plotting at a macro level, reveals a multi-locational formation. Each of her stories is textured on these three narrative stands/voices/trajectories – the folk/subaltern, the modern and the authorial. The first stand of her multi-locational grid emerges out of the folk/the subaltern/the tribal. The evolutionary weave of the subaltern strand is cyclic, natural and organic which is embedded in the thought process/action and vocabulary of the marginal. The folk derive its self-definition with relation to nature.

The folk narrative strand in Mahasweta's stories comes out in its own unique expressive idiom which is conveyed through a raw, passionate language of emotions. Even while it is subjected to the severest of oppressions, the language of the subaltern is informed by a rhythmic, lyrical quality. The organic attachments of the subaltern with its kinsfolk are narrated in a linguistic rhythm that conveys/ corresponds to their warm, loving, tender relations. In *Rudali,* for example, the description of Sanichari's domestic life, of her and her husband's future plans, assumes a certain narrative flow thus: A piece of land has been left to her husband's brother by her father-in-law; together the couple had built a little hut on it. She had painted designs and pictures on the walls. Budhua's father wanted to fence their angan, and grow chillies and vegetables. She had plans to raise a calf she would get from Malik's wife. It was all fixed. Her husband said, 'Come, let's visit the Baisakhi mela at Tohri. We can offer worship to Shiva as well. After all, we've managed to save up seven rupees'!.

While describing their home, the emphasis is on the idea of a shared space; the plural pronouns ('their', 'we', 'us') give a feel of warm companionship and camaraderie. Similarly while narrating Sanichari's mental state at the idea of her son's imminent death, the language of the text takes a sudden turn. The direct, unsentimental recounting of the tale transforms into an intense, metaphorical narration of her inner turmoil: Budhua contracted the wasting fever and hacking cough of tuberculosis. The fever rises at night, and then breaks into a sweat at dawn. There is blood when he coughs, dark shadows under his eyes. Sanichari felt as if the flames of the funeral pyre were burning within her, she felt the scorching heat blowing about her day and night.

Intensely emotional, repetitive sentences convey the mental agony and desperation of the subaltern: That day – not just that day, for several days before that – Budhua's condition has worsened. The vaid's medicine was not working. Sanichari asked her to stay with Budhua. She herself went, running all the way, to ask the vaid for some other medicine. She went even though she knew that no medicine could help him now.

Such a lyrical poignancy of narration marks the folk's interaction not only with blood relations but with the other subalterns who form a sublime bonding on the basis of their shared oppression/exploitation. The language of ordinary communication seems utterly inadequate to convey such bondings and hence the folk narrative takes to language of silent, tactile communication.

The feudal/modern constantly engages into ideological appropriation of the subaltern in the narrative. Jashoda has thoroughly internalised the patriarchal ideology. She believes in traditional sexual division of labour that posits: 'The man brings, the woman cooks and serves'. Such an ideological conviction with which the subaltern is made to identify, gives her a false sense of self-confidence thus: Jashoda became vocal and, constantly suckling the infants, she opined as she sat in the Mistresses room, 'A woman breeds, so here medicine, there blood-pressure, here doctors visits. Showoffs! Look at me! I've become a year-breeder! So is my body failing, or is my milk drying? Makes your skin crawl? I hear they are drying their milk with injishuns. Never heard of such things!'.

The gendered subaltern's absolute hegemonisation is reflected in her unquestioning acquiescence to coercive sexual encounters. Jashoda tells her husband, "You are husband, you are guru. If I forget and say no, correct me. Where after all is the pain? Didn't Mistress Mother breed thirteen? Does it hurt a tree to bear fruit?". Such gendered discourse promotes reproduction as the 'natural' function of women. Such discursive conditioning is instrumental in her reproachful blaming of the granddaughters-in-law for 'causing' the Old Mistress's death through their refusal to bear children: 'Mother!' she laments, 'You are blessed, why should you stay in this sinful world! The daughters-in-law have moved the throne! When the tree says I won't be, alas it's a sin! Could you bear so much sin, Mother! Then did the Lion seated turn her back, Mother! You knew the abode of good works had become the abode of sin, It was not for you Mother!'

The feudal narrative is structured of the politics for hegemonization. It hegemonies the subaltern narrative through appropriation and exploitation of its very own symbols. The narrative of the feudal is permeated throughout by materialistic, neo-colonial values. Mahasweta gives a peep into the decadence of the feudal in the description of the 'exploits' of Haldar's new son-in-law in the beginning of the story. It's one of his whimsical exploits that leads to the crippling of Kangali and Jashoda's consequent entry into professional motherhood. The whims of the feudal decide the destiny of the subaltern. The feudal brutalises the subaltern even as it pays a selective tribute to it. Haldarbabu extravagantly declares his reverence for the Brahmin, "there is no East or West for a Brahmin. If there's a sacred thread around his neck you have to give him respect even when he's taking a shit". His feudal mentality is conditioned by colonial traits of selfishness and a contemptuous attitude to the native. He doesn't trust anyone outside of his native place Harisal. 'He is a successful son of Harisal. When he sees a West Bengali fly he says, 'Tchah! at home even the flies were fat – in the bloody West everything is pinched-skinned'. The feudal is parochial and provincial. Haldarbabu's patriotism obstinately refuses to go beyond Harisal. The inclusion of patriots from other parts of the country in history books vexes him: 'Nonsense! why do they make'em read the lives of characters from Dhaka, Mymensingh, Jashore? Harisal is made of the bone of the martyr God. One day it will emerge that the Vedas and the Upanishads were also written in Harisal'.

The feudal narrativity manipulates the discourse of caste to use it as a tool for the exploitation of the subaltern. While Jashoda's caste makes her services even more desirable at the Haldar house – she is termed as the legendary Cow of Fulfilment, 'The fruitful Brahmin wife', 'Mother of the World', 'Milk Mother' – the same caste-status is turned into her undoing when she contracts the life-threatening disease. Her caste-status necessitates her abandonment as the Haldars 'can't send a Brahmin's daughter to a hospital'; neither can they allow her to die at their house. Jashoda's caste which fetched her ritualistic reverence, leads to her ultimate victimisation. The tender, loving, organic narrative of subaltern bonding sharply contrasts with the harsh, callous, artificial and plastic text of the feudal narrative. Mahasweta contrasts the organic relationships (based upon care and compassion) among the subaltern with the plastic/self-serving bonds dictated by the narrow self-interest existing among the feudal. Her fiction presents a number of telling tales of feudal inhumanity, the relationships among whom are governed by petty financial gains.

Mahasweta's narrative locates the feudal in hypocrisy, pretension and falsehood. The idea of the death of a dear one is bereft of any genuine grief. Their grief is a sham; it is solely governed by hope for material gains. Death is seen as an occasion to show off splendour. Nathuni Singh is not willing to spend a paisa on trying to cure his mother, but plans to spend thirty thousand on her funeral. His middle wife doesn't want to be left behind, being the daughter of a wealthier father she avows: 'May my father live long – but when he dies, then I'll show everyone how a kriya should be held! Mahasweta Devi, thus, draws a parallel between the folk and the feudal to highlight the contrast in the very fundamentals of their living and location, their existence and emotion. The emotions of the feudal have dried up due to greed, corrupt morals, absence of humanity; those of the folk have dried up due to hunger, poverty, starvation. The feudal doesn't grieve as the hope for financial gain is more real and immediate. The folk are disallowed to grieve by the more immediate worries for survival: After the worst disasters people gradually bathe, eat, chase away the goat nibbling the chillies in the yard. People can do anything – but if they can't eat, they die. If Sanichari has survived so much grief, she'll survive the loss of Bhikni. She's devastated, but she won't cry. Money, rice, new clothes – without getting these in return, tears are a useless luxury'.

The moral bankruptcy of the feudal is juxtaposed with the folk disbelief of such moral corruption. The simple, sincere, honest, subaltern is unable to comprehend the upper class pretensions. Hearing of Nathuni Singh's callousness, Sanichari exclaims with disbelief, "My God, and his mother's not even dead yet!".

A singular feature of Mahasweta's text, thus, is the comparative critique of the feudal-modern location that runs throughout the narrative. In Rudali, an overt criticism of the upper-caste politics of hegemony and hypocrisy is presented by Mahasweta through the subaltern and at places through the narratorial voice.

In *Rudali*, most of such criticism comes from Dulan whose satirical statements lay bare the upper-caste vanity. "In rich families the son kills the mother, the mother kills the son. Forget about who killed whom. Amongst us, when someone dies, we all mourn. Amongst the rich, family members are too busy trying to find the keys to the safe".

Exposing the callousness of the feudal, he says, "their whole attitude is topsy-turvy. They don't care about the living, but once they're dead they hold grand funerals and try to raise their prestige".

Always reeling under existential pressures, the subaltern, in most of Mahasweta's stories, enters and gets hegemonized by the mainstream narrative by internalising the very discourse aimed at controlling and marginalising them. However, Rudali presents an exception as here, in this story, the subaltern is continuously aware of the power structures operating around her/him and hence she/he doesn't completely lose her agency even as she/he enters the hegemonising system.

Mahasweta constructs the character of Dulan to convey such subtle interface between the feudal and subaltern narrative locations. The subalterns in Rudali are controlled, but not hegemonized. Dulan's satirical scathing statements reveal his political awareness and serve to politicise other subalterns like Sanichari and Bhikni. The character of Dulan forms a significant aspect of Mahasweta's narrative strategy as it serves to add a new dimension of a knowing manipulative subaltern to her folk narrative. With such a politicisation of the subaltern location, Mahasweta invests them with a certain cunningness that aids them in their struggle for survival. The folk narrative in Rudali is dotted with such instances where the subaltern employs trickery to nudge in a space for survival. Dulan suggests Bhikni and Sanichari who come to take his counsel to employ the discourse of religion to fetch them a living: pick up a nice stone from the banks of Kuruda river . . . anoint it with oil and sindoor and proclaim that Mahabirji had come . . . in my dreams . . . present yourself and Mahabirji at the Tohri marketplace. Collect offerings from the devout'.

The subaltern response to the harsh conditions afflicting her/his life is characterised by pragmatic, practical wisdom. Mahasweta envisages knowledge, awareness and pragmatism as the weapons through which the folk can counter the hegemonizing feudal discourse and expand its location. Dulan tries to convince Sanichari with his pragmatic reasoning, "if your mind is pure, the Ganga flows even through wood. Look here, Budhua's ma, there is no bigger god than one's belly. For the belly's sake everything is permissible".

In fact, the character of Dulan serves an important narrative function. Mahasweta attempts to purge the popular narrative of its conventional conservatism by positioning the pragmatic Dulan at the centre of the marginalised narrative location. Under Mahasweta's activist agenda of qualifying the folk narrative by stripping it off its narrow-mindedness and blind prejudices, Dulan functions as a seasonal subaltern strategist. Mahasweta's attribution of rationality to the folk lends the popular narrative a more liberating character than that of the feudal-modern. The folk is envisioned as far more radical than feudal as it refuses to recognize the morality that blocks survival. Dulan's rational argumentation attempts to break the popular resistance rooted in convention by establishing that the prostitutes too deserved an equal treatment, since they too were like other low-caste women, wronged and victimized by the Malik-Mahajans. The character of Dulan serves the purpose of an 'organic intellectual' in *Rudali* who refuses to recognize the moral structures that come in the way to survival.

He advocates a discarding of false morality by positing the ethics and morality to be sheer luxury as against the question of survival: 'Don't weigh right and wrong so much, leave that kind of thing to the rich. They understand it better. We understand hunger ... What one is forced to do to feed oneself is never considered wrong'. Dulan embodies Mahasweta's vision as it redefines the conventional discourse of morality by repeatedly stressing that funeral wailing, prostitution, neither of these is low work. Without having these pass through the moral filter, Mahasweta places funeral wailing, prostitution on an equal pedestal with other kinds of production labour by positing all of these as labour-for-a-living. Such an ethical stance of the author gets buttressed when one hears the echoes of false, pretentious, hypocritical morality of the upper-class narrative as a contrast.

The subaltern attempts to create a livable space through an ironic subversion of the Rudali custom. Sanichari not only survives, but emerges stronger, freer, and empowered enough to control her situation. Subaltern creates her space by employing the very distortion of emotions which is forced on her by the circumstances to invert the oppressive system. Mahasweta's overarching vision seeks to give the subaltern a chance to nudge out a livable space by hinting at the possibility of subversion and re-ordering of the exploitative super structure. Though Mahasweta takes sides, she doesn't present a final solution. There is a continuous postponement of a single final solution as the complex trajectories of lives and situations demand to be resolved through equally complex ways.

Yet another aspect of Mahasweta's narrative is rooted in feudal/modern narrative location which, by contrast, is linear, rational and fragmentary. Senanayak of *Draupadi* epitomises this narrative trajectory most appropriately of all Mahasweta's characters. He embodies the modern, rational pragmatism which entails an absolute compartmentalization of theory and practice: 'whatever his practice, in theory he respects the opposition'. In practice, he aims to destroy the enemy but in theory, he becomes one with them in order to understand them. In practice, 'he is getting rid of the young' by means of 'apprehension and elimination'; while in theory, he 'believes in delivering the world's legacy into youth's hands'. In theory, he preaches the 'soldierly' skills to Arjan Singh and others; in practice, he orders the hunter's way for the enemy's capture because he knows that the enemy 'can't be dispatched by the approved method'.

In most of the Mahasweta's narratives, exocitisation, eroticization and homogenization of the subaltern are common exploitative planks of the modern narrative. Jashoda is exoticised as the 'Legendary Cow of Fulfilment' due to her "flooding"/overflowing breasts; Gangor's breasts are eroticized as aesthetic objects of photography.

Such an essentialized construction of the tribal/subaltern places them in reductionist paradigms whereby they are perceived either as idealised, superhuman/supernatural beings or as savage representatives of evil. The mainstream male narrative that functions through a delimiting perception of the subaltern, aims to project it as a dehumanised entity. The tribal naxalite revolutionary Dopdi, for Senanayak, instead of being a human problem, is a law and order problem.

The homogenising, rational modern narrative is invariably characterised by prosaic, linear, synthetic worldview. As opposed to the non-hierarchical harmonising organic attachment of the folk to nature, the modern perceives nature as the challenging other which needs to be domesticated to advance their culture. Since, the tribal coexists as a part of nature, such a culturization of nature entails a Civilization of the tribal subaltern as well.

The authorial voice inserts itself in each of her stories in a distinct way, somewhere it enters in the form of mass media, somewhere in the form of objective language of cold analysis, at places it exhibits itself in emotional outbursts, at still other places it comes embodied in any of the characters of the story. This authorial voice, in whatever form it emerges in the narrative, is always aimed at corrective critique/questioning. Such a critical narrative standpoint is grounded in the critical tropes of irony, inversion and subversion.

The omnipresence and authority of such a narrative stance is visible in the way Mahasweta Devi negotiates with the folk and feudal-modern narratives. It filters the folk through its lens of irony, as in the description of Jashoda: Jashoda is fully an Indian woman, whose unreasonable, unreasoning, and unintelligent devotion to her husband and love for her children, whose unnatural renunciation and forgiveness have been kept alive in the popular consciousness by all Indian women from Sati-Savitri-Sita. The creeps of the world understand by seeing such women that the old Indian tradition is still flowing free – they understand that it was with such women in mind that the following aphorisms have been composed – 'A female's life hangs on like a turtle's' – 'her heart breaks but no word is uttered' – 'the woman will burn, her ashes will fly/ Only then will we sing her/praise on high.' Frankly, Jashoda never once wants to blame her husband for her present misfortunes. Her mother-love wells up Kangali as much as for the children. She wants to become the earth and feed her crippled husband and helpless children with a fulsome harvest.

Such a strong authorial intervention serves to hold the folk and the feudal narratives in perspective. Through derisive descriptions of Jashoda and her profession, the authorial narrative heightens the irony of the subaltern's fate. The entire narrative reads like a satiric exposure of the religious gendered ideologies where the feudal is satirically located in the discourses of hypocrisy and hegemony.

The narrative voice's satirical conduct of the feudal-modern subverts the self-proclaimed modernity of such narratives. The authorial digressions expose the hypocrisy written within the paternalistic discourse of the national elite: 'Such is the power of the Indian soil that all women turn into mothers here and all men remain immersed in the spirit of holy childhood. Each man the Holy Child and each woman the Divine Mother. She widens the scope of her narrative as she moves on to criticise the hypocrisy of the Indian male intellectuals who professedly value female liberation. The narrator comments: Even those who deny this and wish to slap current posters to the effect of the 'eternal she' – 'Mona Lisa'- 'La Passionaria' – 'Simone de Beauvoir,' et cetera, over the old ones and look at women the way they are, after all, Indian cubs. It is notable that the educated Babus desire all these from women outside the home. When they cross the threshold they want the Divine Mother in the words and conduct of the revolutionary ladies. The feudal while it performs ritualistic observances, like Mr. Haldar 'would touch the feet of Kangali, young enough to be his son, and put a pinch of dust from his chapped feet on his own tongue' and is duly worried at the thought of Kangali's feet, being turned to ground meat as 'he would not be able to taste their dust', it is actually oblivious to the plight of the subaltern. The mainstream bourgeoisie, who pride themselves on the proper reverence for the Brahmin, refuse to take responsibility to improve the life of the impoverished. A trivialised appeal to the tradition satisfies their spiritual needs. The narrative of the feudal is deeply embedded in self-interest. The Haldars agree to employ Jashoda not due to a sense of ethical responsibility, but because the second son insightfully perceives a way in Jashoda's milk to preserve his wife's beauty while propagating more children on her body. "Way found", he exults, as he reveals his divine discovery to his wife. With the death of the older generation of Haldars, Jashoda loses her employment as the Haldar daughters-in-law leave the household and take off to the workplaces of their husbands. The assistance of Jashoda, the Haldar women move out of patriarchal control into a kind of reproductive emancipation. Jashoda, the proletarian, is useful to them at the initial stage in giving them freedom from the reproductive fear, when this usefulness ends, she is discarded. The proletarian is abused and then discarded by the bourgeoisie. The bourgeois women equally contribute to the subalternization of another set of women as represented by Jashoda.

A notable feature of the story is that while the subaltern female has internalised and refuses to come out of the mythical, stereotypical, patriarchal binds, the bourgeois female breaks such binding discourses under the modernist winds of nationalism. The narrative of nationalism results in further marginalisation of Jashoda as she becomes a stepping stone for the emancipation of the mainstream females.

Despite her critique of both, Mahasweta does not create clear-cut binaries in terms of narrative locations. The patriarchy, for example, dominates the gendered. Both the subaltern and the elite women are conditioned by patriarchal ideology; both take their repeated pregnancies as an act of God. But the bourgeoisie women are shown to be far more aware in terms of their consciousness for their health and beauty. The wife of the second son of the Haldar house retorts when her husband proposes to save her the pain, "how? I'll be out of pain when you burn me. Can a year-breeder's health mend?". They are pleased to find a way to keep themselves in "blouses and bras of European Cut". There is a definite progression towards increased reproductive freedom in successive generations of Haldar women while the subaltern remains entrenched in the hegemonizing patriarchal ideology.

Similarly the text punctures the elite-subaltern binary by contextualising its polarities. The discourse of the religion figures prominently in both the narratives. Both of these subscribe to religious orthodoxy and attempt to manoeuvre it for personal gains. Nabin advises Kangalicharan to make a Hare Krishna racket to eke out a living. He also explains the simple, straight procedure for it: "Get a Gopal in your dream. My aunt brought a stony Gopal from Puri. I give it to you. You announce that you got it in a dream. You'll see there'll be a to-do in no time, money will roll in. start for money, later you'll get devoted to Gopal".

Conditioning of the target audience is one of the salient features of Mahasweta's creations. She employs various strategies – some of which have been discussed already – to condition her target audience. Two of these include – direct intervention in the narrative, and invention of an idiom that is not only commensurate with the articulation of the subaltern voice but also helps the reader to identify with the plight of the subject of the narrative.

Mahasweta's stories reveal certain common nodes and therefore seem to merge into each other. Her narratives when taken together as a whole come out as nuanced and evolving studies of similar thematic from different vantage positions. The repetition, if any, is to be traced in her thematic concerns and must be attributed to her activist aim of bringing the mechanics of subalternation/marginalisation to light and thus achieving audience conditioning that serves to fulfil the duty of a socially responsible art.

A deeper probe into the supposed commonality of her stories reveals a definite progression in the evolution of Mahasweta's activist worldview and her solutions. The endings of her stories, when studied on a chronological scale, correspond to the trajectory of India as a nation in their progression. The seemingly simple, linear narratives which terminate into closed endings in the earlier phase of her writing evolve into ambivalent 186 and ambiguous, open- ended constructions in the later phase of her career. This progression metaphorical the phases in the development of the construct of nation which evolved from a homogenous, monolithic, unilinear concept to a cacophonous, diffused entity incorporating tensions and collisions within its ambit, in its later phases. Such an evolution of Mahasweta's narratives can be traced in a successive progression of her characters. Her characters seem to pass through an evolutionary trajectory as they parallel the process of 'serial-ization' in her successive stories.

Mahasweta's entire creative oeuvre can be read in terms of an extended story of composite Indian womanhood and its evolution through time. Sanichari, Dopdi, Jashoda – these are not distinct women rather all these come together to chart out the progress of woman who is a mute witness to her exploitation, whose position of total submission transforms into a resisting acceptance of exploitative condition, which metamorphoses into a flouting of socially-sanctioned male narrative position of a guilt-ridden, miserable sexually exploited/betrayed woman that ultimately explodes into a revolting /rebellious woman who totally shatters the androcentric stereotype of a raped woman. Her woman thus passes through the trajectory of evolution and charts a definite progression towards a composite womanhood.

Such an evolutionary process that characterises Mahasweta's creative oeuvre serves to break the expectation stereotypes at every level as it constantly expands her thematic with innovations and therefore effectively re-orients the response of its readers. Mahasweta's activist strategy to empower the subaltern is conveyed as much through the linguistic means as through the narrative. She ruptures the linguistic structures/canons of mainstream literature. Mahasweta manipulates the standard linguistic expectations to transform the subaltern acts, articulations, and responses into the tools of strength and self-respect minus servility and self-denigration.

Through a persistent focus on the protagonist's body-language, as is obvious in the above narrative vignettes, Mahasweta aims to reproduce the total communicative personality of Dopdi/her subject. Strong, power-packed verbs in present tense invest the gendered subaltern with the power to reverse the subject-object hierarchies. Draupadi's actions – she comes walking with her body upright and head held high, she stands with her hands akimbo, she comes closer and laughs loudly, she speaks in a terrifying voice, she spits blood on Senanayak, she pushes Senanayak with her breasts – captured in a language that conveys their full physical force, sharply contrast with the brief sentences describing the position of Senanayak vis-à-vis Draupadi as he stands before her to encounter her: Senanayak walked out surprised and sees Draupadi, naked.Walking towards him.

This linguistic strategy where Mahasweta Devi entrusts language with the task to empower her subaltern subjects is a consistent feature of her aesthetic enterprise.

In *Draupadi*, the scene of police violence is brought alive with a corresponding violence of certain brutally candid images thus: By the law of confrontation [they are shot] their eyeballs, intestines, stomachs, hearts, genitals, and soon become the food of fox, vulture, hyena, wildcat, ant, and worm and the untouchables go off happily to sell their bare skeletons. After confrontations ... the skeletons discovered with arms broken or severed? ... armless men ... collarbones shake ... legs and ribs crushed? Even her metaphors are geared towards the same end and blend uncannily with her purpose. The 'Operation', for example, to trace Dopdi in the forest belt of Jharkhani is a 'Carbuncle' on the government's backside. Not to be cured by the tested ointment, not to burst with the appropriate herb'. The soldiers climb the trees and embrace leafy boughs like 'so many great God pans and wait as the large red ants bite their private parts'. At many places, Mahasweta uses localised metaphors, for example Draupadi's association with the primitive world gets strengthened in the comparison of her suspicion with hedgehog's hair: 'Spines of suspicion are always furled in her mind. Hearing 'Dopdi' they stiffen like a hedgehog's'.

In the story of professional mother Jashoda (*Breast Giver*), Mahasweta reinscribes mythic Yashoda as well as the very connotations of the word 'mother'. She qualifies the semantics associated with the word "mother" through repetition and invests into it the economies of commercial exchange – 'Motherhood was always her way of living ... Jashoda was a mother by profession, professional mother. Jashoda was not an amateur mama ... Jashoda had taken motherhood as her profession'.

In Mahasweta's works, content is more important than the form or technique. The aesthetic organisation of her art is determined by the content instead of the form. Her aesthetic is born out of the disturbing moral-political activist agenda that is at the core of her entire artistic oeuvre/enterprise.

The role of description in a women's narrative gains significance as women writers, unlike men, use description as a technique. Descriptive passages in Ambai and Mahasweta Devi are short and purposeful and form a part of their narrative. They cannot be detached and enjoyed for their own sake or whisked away from the text without damaging its fabric. Besides, they are closer to the meaning of the text.

Using these literary devices- imagery-symbol-satires, irony and description- Ambai and Mahasweta Devi triggers at once a multiplicity of associations to express her multiple experiences.

The amount of work done by a homemaker is a matter of debate in the Indian context, as it is taken for granted by the men. A homemaker's work may not be financially rewarding, yet it must be considered as precious. Without this tedious physical work, a house can never become home.

References

Ahuja, Neel. "Postcolonial Critique in a Multispecies World." PMLA 124.2 (Mar 2009): 556-563.

Ambai. a purple sea. Trans. Lakshmi Holmstrom. Chennai: East West Books (Madras) Pvt. Ltd, 2004.

--- Ambai ciRukataikal (1972- 2000) . Nagercoil: Kalachuvadu Pathippagam, 2007.

Anantharaman, Latha. Rev. of A Purple Sea: Short Stories. The India Magazine 18.1 (December 1997): 66- 67.

Anwar,Waseem. "Transcribing Resistence: Cartographies of Struggling Bodies and Minds in Mahasweta Devi's Imaginary Maps." South Asian Review 22. (December 2001): 83-96.

Aruna, A Marie Josephine. "The Socio- Political Philosophy of Life in Mahasweta Devi's Old Women." Contemporary Vibes 5.20 (Jul-Sep 2010): 12-14.

Asaduddin, M. "Of Rape and Marginalization." Rev. of 1. Outcast: Four Stories by Mahasweta Devi, Translated into English by Sarmistra Dutta Gupta and 2. The Book of the Hunter. The Book Review 26.11 (November 2002): 34-35.

Ashokamitran. "Thinking changes too." Rev. of A Purple Sea: Short Stories. Indian Review of Books 1.11 (Aug 1992): 27.

Bail, Scharada. Icons of Social Change. New Delhi: Penguin Books India, 2004. Xii, 130.

Balachandran, K. Critical Essays on Canadian Literature. New Delhi: Sarup & Sons, 2003. Xvii,162.

Bande, Usha. "Women Writers with Fire in their Pen." Cyber Literature 2.1 (Aug 1998):19-24.

Basu, Lopamudra. "Mourning and Motherhood: transforming loss in representations of Adivasi Mothers in Mahasweta Devi's Short Stories." South Asian Review 28.4 (2007): 9.

Basu, Chitralekha. "Women Unlimited." Rev. of Katha. The Times Literary Supplement 5490 (Jun 20 2008): 20

Beniwal, Anup and Vandana. "Writing the Subaltern at the Interface of Fiction and Idealogy : an engagement with the works of Mahasweta Devi's Fiction." The Quest 21.1 (Jun 2007): 25-44.

Bhattacharya, Pradip. "The Story is The Thing." Rev .of. 1. The Mahabharata of Vyasa: The Complete Adi Parva Trans. From Sanskrit by P.Lal 2. The Mahabharata BY Meera Uberoi 3. After Kurukshetra by Mahasweta Devi. The Book Review 30.1-2(Jan-Feb 2006): 31-33.

Bhattacharya, Nirmal Kanti. "Oeuvre of a Socially Committed Literateur." Rev. of Mahasweta Devi: an anthology of recent criticism. The Book Review 33.6 (Jun 2009): 28-29.

Bhatnagar, Sandeep. "Literature With a Mission." Rev. of Bitter Soil: Stories. Indian Review of Books 8.4 (16 Jan- 15 Feb 1999): 41-42.

Chakraborty, Madhurima. "Dangerous Memories: social justice and the politics of the present in Mahasweta Devi's Statue." South Asian Review 28.4(2007): 13-14.

Chakraborty, Madhurima. "Dangerous Memories: social justice and the politics of the present in Mahasweta Devi's Statue." South Asian Review 30.2(Oct-Nov 2009): 211-224.

Chakravarty, Saumitra. "Understanding the Forest and its Resources: Mahasweta Devi's Campaign Against Colonization of Tribal Habitat." Littcrit 34.2 – 66 (Dec 2008): 15-25.

Chakraborty, Urmila. "Art as Protest: Social Commitment in the Novels of Mahasweta Devi", Indian Women Novelists: Set III: Vol.7. R.K.Dhawan (Ed.) New Delhi: Prestige Booka, 1995. 159- 176.

Chari,A.Jaganmohana. "Deconstructing History: A Study of Mahasweta's Imaginary Maps." Revalutions 3.1 (Summer 1997): 54-75.

Chari,A.Jaganmohana and E.Satyanarayana. "The Dramatic Strategies in Mahasweta Devi's Five Plays." Kakatiya Journal of English Studies 18(1998): 157-163.

Chatterjee, Enakshi. "In Splendid Isolation: Enakshi Chatterjee pays tribute to Mahasweta Devi, Winner of the 1996 Jnanpith AWARD." INDIAN Review of Books 6.9 (16 Jun- 15 Jul 1997): 4- 5.

Chatterjee, M.N. Rev. of Three Sides of Life: short stories. Indian Literature 52.2 – 244 (Mar- Apr 2008): 172-175.

Chatterjee, M.N. "Re-reading of Mahasweta Devi." Rev. of Mahasweta Devi: an anthology of recent criticism. Indian Literature 52.6 – 248 (Nov- Dec 2008): 239-240.

Chatterjee, Maitreyi, "Three Faces of Eve." Rev. of Rudali. The Book Review 18.12 (Dec 1994): 20.

Chaudhuri, Supriya. "Narratives of Endurance." Rev. of 1. The Stream Within: Short Stories by Contemporary Bengali Women Translated by Swati

Ganguly and Sarmistha Dutta Gupta, 2. Old Women. The Book Review 23.7 (July 1999): 29-30.

Chew, Shirley. Rev. of Chotti Munda and His Arrow. WASAFIRI 40 (Winter 2003): 58-59.

Collu, Gabrielle. "Adivasis and the Myth of Independence: Mahsweta Devi's "Douloti the Boubtiful"." Ariel 30.1 (January 1999): 43- 57.

Dasan, A.S. "The Subaltern as Metaphor: a dialogic reading of Mahasweta Devi's Breast Stories." Littcrit 34.2- 66 (Dec 2008): 76- 90.

Dasan, M. "Writer as Fighter:Concern for Human Rights Violations in Mahasweta Devi's Plays." The Commonwealth Review 13.1: 128- 138.

Dasan, M. "Writer as Fighter:Concern for Human Rights Violations in Mahasweta Devi's Plays." The Literary Criterion 40.2 (2005): 42- 52.

Dasgupta, Subha Chakraborty. "Contesting Polarities: Creating Spaces – Reading Myths in Mahasweta Devi's Stories." Indian Literature 47.2 (March-April 2003): 200- 205.

Devi, Mahasweta. After Kurukshetra: Three Stories. Calcutta: Seagull, 2005.

---Breast Stories. Trans. Gayatri Chakravorty Spivak. Calcutta: Seagull, 2010.

---Rudali. Trans. Anjum Katyal. Calcutta: Seagull, 2010.

---Old Women. Trans. Gayatri Chakravorty Spivak. Calcutta: Seagull, 2008.

Devi, Mahasweta. Tarasankar Bandyopadhyay. New Delhi: Sahitya Akademi, 1983. 79.

Devi, Mahasweta. "Tarasankar's World of Changes and the New Order." Indian Literature 12.1 (Mar 1969): 71- 79.

Devi, Mahasweta. "Untapped Resources." Seminar: Literature and Society 359 (Jul 1989): 15- 19.

Devi, Mahasweta. ""I am Interested in History"." Kakatiya Journal of English Studies 18. (1998): 93- 99.

Devi, Mahasweta. ""Jyotirmoyee Devi: In the Light of a Hundred Years"." The Book Review 22.9 (September 1998): 31- 32.

Devy, Ganesh N. "The Adivasi Mahasweta." Littcrit 34.2 – 66 (Dec 2008): 5- 14.

Dilip D'Souza in Rediff on the Net. On the death of Budhan Sabar. http://www.rediff.com/news/1999/jun/10dilip.htm

Dutta, Kalyani. "Battling for the People: Mahasweta Devi." Pratibha India 14.3 (Apr-Jun 1995): 3, 5- 6.

Dutta, Kalyani. Rev. of A Purple Sea. Pratibha India 11.4 (Jul- Sep 1992): 48- 49.

Finding Justice with Arundhati Roy Terence McNally interviews Arundhati Roy on her activism and shift from novel writing to addressing the public on globalization and neocolonialism for AlterNet. Posted September 21,2004. http://www.alternet.org/story/19936

Ghanshyam, G.A. "I Was Ever a Fighter, So- One Fight More: Dalit's Voice from the Margin." Writers Editors Critics 1.1 (Mar 2011): 86- 95.

Ghosh, Shoba Venkatesh. "Refiguring Myth – Draupadi and Three Indian Women Writers." New Quest 116 (Mar- Apr 1996): 91- 98.

Ghosh, Shoba Venkatesh. "Reading Resistance." New Quest 128 (Mar- Apr 1998): 69- 76.

Gill, Gagan. "The business of mourning." Rev. of. 1. Mother of 1084 and 2. Rudali. Biblio: A Review of Books 3. 9-10 (Sep- Oct 1997): 30.

G.N.Devy after the first National Convention of Nomads and Adivasis, May 23, 2005. http://www.indiatogether.org/opinions/edits/

G.N.Devy on the emergence of the history of the Denotified Tribes of India. PUCL Bulleyin, September 1998. http//www.puct.org/from-archives/ Dalit-tribal/branded-tribes.htm

Holmstrom, Lakshmi. "Some Women's Voices in Modern Tamil Literature." The India Magazine 15.8 and 9 (Jul- Aug 1995): 54-58.

Hussein, Aamer. "India's Mother Tongue." Rev. of A Purple Sea. The Times Literary Supplement 4704 (May 28 1993): 24.

Jagannathan, N.S. "A Million Faces of Gender Oppression." Rev. of Veetu Moolayil Oru Samayalarai: (Tamil). The Book Review 14.1 (Jan- Feb 1990): 39-40.

Jagannathan, N.S. "Champion of the Downtrodden." Rev. of Dust on the Road: The Activist Writings of Mahasweta Devi. Indian Review of Books 7.5 (16 Feb-15 Mar 1998): 11-12.

Jaidev. "This Fiction is Injurious to Illusions." Rev. of Mother of 1084 and Breast Stories. Indian Review Books 6.9 (16 Jun-15 Jul 1997); 5-9.

Jaidev. "But Trees, Alas, Do Not Saris Grow." Rev. of Dust on the Road: The Activist Writings of Mahasweta Devi. Indian Book Chronivle 23.11 (November 1998): 5-7.

Jaidev. "Douloti as a National Allegory." Kakatiye Journal of English Studies 18. (1998): 133- 150.

Jaidev. "Against 'So What's." Rev. of A Purple Sea: Short Stories. Indian Review of Books 7.2 (16 Nov- 15 Dec 1997): 48- 50.

Jain,Jasbir. "The Feminist Perspective: The Indian Situation and its Literary Manifestations", Problems of Postcolonial Literatures and Other Essays. Jasbir Jain. Jaipur: Printwell Publishers. 1991.29- 39.

Jamuna,B.S. "Voicing the Voiceless: the criterion of authenticity and audibility of Subalternity in the Plays of Mahasweta Devi". Littcrit 34.2- 66 (Dec 2008): 137- 146.

Janaky. "Stuff of Legends." Rev. of Titu Mir. Indian Review of Books 9.9 (June 16-July 15 2000): 32-34.

Karlekar, Malavika. Rev. of 1. Mother of 1084 by Mahasweta Devi, Translated with an introduction essay by Samik Bandyopadhyay, 2. Rudali- From Fiction to Performance by Mahasweta Devi and Usha Gaguli, Translated with an introductory essay by Anjum Katyal. 3. Five Plays by Mahasweta Devi, Translated by Samik Bandyopadhyay and 4.Breast Stories. Indian Journal of Gender Studies 5.1 (January- June 1998): 137-144.

Kannan, Lakshmi. "Scripting Her Life." Rey. Of Ambai: Two Novellas and a story. The Book Review 27.8 (August 2003): 35.

Katyal, Anjum. " A Coming Toghter; An Affirmation; A Sharing Kulavai : A Report." Segull Theatre quarterly 9 (April 1996):41-53.

Katyal, Anjum. "The Metamorphoses of Rudali." Seagull Theatre Quarterly 1 (January 1994): 5- 11.

Kaul, Ranjana. "Individual in History." Rev. of Titu Mir. The Book Review 25.2 (February 2001):33.

Kaul, Ranjana. "Silences in Women's Lives." Rev. of Ambai. The Book Review 24. 1-2 (January – February 2000): 74- 75.

Khan, Nazneen. "Defiant Militant Heroines: a study of Naugi wa Thiong'O's The Trial of Dedan Kimathi and Mahasweta Devi's Draupadi." Dialogue 6.1 (Jun 2010):63- 70.

Krishanan, Lakshmi. "Gaze as a Device in Fiction." The Commonwealth Review 16.2" 312- 330.

Mahanand, Anand. "Re- Visioning History: Mahaseta Devi's Aranyer Adhikar." Kakatiye Journal of English Studies 18. (1998): 151- 156.

Mahanta, Banibrata. "The Subaltern as Subject: rading Mahasweta Devi's After Kurukshetra." Dialogue 2.1 (Jun 2006): 24-34.

Majumdar, Nivedita. "The Nation and its Outcastes: a reading of Mahasweta Devi's Douloti the Bountiful." South Asian Review 30.2 (Oct- Nov 2009): 153- 166.

Mani, Jessy. "Narrating the Nation from Gendered Locations." The Commonwealth Review 17.1:82- 92.

Mathi,S. Nirai. "Mahasweta Devi, The Rebel Playwright of Mother of 1084." The Literary Criterion 42.3 and 4 (2007): 33- 36.

Mukherjee, Sujit. "Mahasweta Devi's Writings- An Evaluation." Rev. of Bashai Tudu. The Book Review 15.3 (May- June 1991): 30-31.

Nair, Bindu. "Subversion and Resistance: the uses of Myth in Mahasweta Devi are The Hunt and The Book of the Hunter." Littcrit 34.2- 66 (Dec 2008): 111- 119.

Nair, Vijay. "Receptive and Explorative Social Character Types in Mahasweta Devi's Aajir." Littcrit 34.2- 66 (Dec 2008): 132- 136.

Nandakumar, Prema. " A Soul on Fire." Rev. of A Purple Sea: Short Stories. Indian Book Chronicle 20.5 (May 1995): 15.

Nandakumar, Prema. Rev. of A Purple Sea. World Literature Today 68.1 (Win 1994): 213- 214.

Narasimhan, Raji. " A Telescopic Arousal of Time." Rev. of A Purple Sea. The Book Review 16.6 (Nov – Dec 1992): 29- 30.

Noor, Ronny. Rev . of Old Women: Statue and the Fairy Tale of Mohanpur. World Literature Today 74.2 (Spring 2000): 356-357.

Oommen, Susan. "Dharma: After Kurukshetra." Samyukta 7.2 (July 2007): 110- 116.

Pandian K.Raja Ram and R. M alathy. Facets of Ambai. Virudhunagar: Ramal Publications, 2009. Iv, 172.

Panjikaran, Mariamma. "Old Women: a Geropsychological Mosaic." Littcrit 34.2- 66 (Dec2008): 91- 95.

Parameswari, D. Politics of Survival: Studies in Canadian Literature. Madurai: Jane Publishers, 1999.214.

Parameswaran, Uma. Rev. of 1. Five Plays, 2. Mother of 1084 and 3. Breast Stories. World Literature Today 72.2 (Spring 1998): 457-458.

Philip, Ashely. "Aesthetics of Incommunicability: a study of Mahasweta Devi's pterodactyl, Puran Sahay, and Pirtha." Littcrit 34.2 -66 (Dec 2008): 120- 131.

Prasad, Amar Nath. Indian Women Novelists in English. New Delhi: Atlantic Publishers and Distributors, 20001. Xii, 180.

Rajan, Rajeawari Sunder. "Accessing Contemporary Writers." Rev. of The Wordsmiths. The Book Review 20.10 (October 1996): 35.

Ramadevi, A. "Awakening of an Apolitical Mother: Mahasweta Devi's Mother of 1084". The Commonwealth Review 13.1: 139-143.

Rani, T.Jyothi and K.Katyayani. "Violence on women in the Context of Indian Polyical Economy – A Study of Mahasveta Devi's Sri Sri Ganesh

Mahima and Draupadi." Kakatiya Journal of English Studies 18. (1998): 123-132.

Rao, B.Gopal and S. A nanda Babu. "The Image of Emerging New Woman in Mahasweta Devi's Fiction." Kakatiya Journal of English Studies 27. (2007-08): 168- 175.

Rekha. "The Poetics and Politics of Space: a reading of Mahasweta Devi's Subaltern Stories." Indian Literature 54.6-260 (Nov- Dec 2010): 143-160.

Rekhaand Anup Beniwal. "From Re- Presentation to Self- Presentation: the problematic of female body / sexuality in contemporary Indian Women Writing." Littcrit 32.1 and 2 (Jun, Dec 2006): 79-90.

Rekhaand Anup Beniwal. "From Re- Presentation: the problematic of female body / sexuality in contemporary Indian Women Writing." Littcrit 32.1 and 2 (Jun, Dec 2006): 79-90.

Rose, M. Leema. "Narrative Resistance: a reading of Mahasweta Devi's Draupadi." Littcrit 34.2- 66 (Dec 2008): 96- 102.

Roy, Anita. Rev. of The Wordsmiths. The Indian Magazine 17.1 (December 1996): 79-80.

Roy, Nlianjana S. "The Complete Mahasweta." Rev. of Till Death Do Us Part. The Book Review 26.2 (February 2002): 35.

Salgado, Minoli. "Tribal Stories, Scribal Worlds: Mahasweta Devi and the Unreliable Translator." The Journal of Commonwealth Literature 35.1 (2000): 131-145.

Sarada, T. "Lifetime Achievement Award Acceptance Speech by Ambai: translated from the Original Tamizh." Journal of the School of Languages, Literature and Culture Studies 14 New Series (Aut 2010): 69- 72.

Satyanarayana, E. The Plays of Mahasweta Devi. New Delhi: Prestige Books, 2000. 142.

Satyanarayana, E. "Mothers in Mahasweta Devi's mother of 1084 and Bayen", Indian Literature Today: Vol. I: Drama and Fiction. R.K.Dhawan (Ed.) New Delhi: Prestige Books, 1994.53-60.

Satyanarayana, E. "Subaltern Voices: A Note on Women in Mahasweta Devi's Five Plays." Kakatiya Journal of English Studies 15. (Dec 1995): 79-87.

Satyanarayana, E. "Mothers in Mahasweta Devi's Plays Mother of 1084 and Bayen." Kakatiya Journal of English Studies 13. (1993): 138- 146.

Satyanarayana, E. "Mothers in Mahasweta Devi's Plays Mother of 1084 and Bayen."The Commonwealth Review 5.1 (1993- 94): 53- 60.

Satyanarayana, E. "Mahasweta Devi's Urvshi O Johnny: The rebel as artist." The Commonwealth Review 13.1 (1993- 94): 144- 160.

REFERENCES

Satyanarayana, E. "The Unconquered: A Study Of Mahasweta Devi's " Draupadi"" , Indian Women Novelists: Set. III: Vol. 7.. R.K.Dhawan (Ed.) New Delhi: Prestige Books, 1995. 177- 184.

Satyanarayana, E. "Revolt Myth inMahasweta Devi's Operation-? Bashai Tudu" , Indian Women Novelists: Set. III: Vol. 7.. R.K.Dhawan (Ed.) New Delhi: Prestige Books, 1995. 185- 194.

Sekher, Ajay S. "Writing and Agency: a minor critique of Mahasweta Devi's Narration." Littcrit 34.2 – 66 (Dec 2008): 63- 75.

Sen, Nivedita and Nikhail Yadav, Mahasweta Devi: An Anthology of Recent Criticism. New Delhi: 2008. 256.

Sharma, Meenakshi. " The Crafting Years", The Wordsmiths. Meenakshi Sharma (Ed). New Delhi : Katha, 1996. 194- 195.

Singh, Anita. Indian English Novel in the Nineties and After: A Study of the Text and its Context. Delhi: Adhyayan Publishers & Distributors, 2004. Vi, 155.

Singh, Malvika. Freeing the Spirit: The Iconic Women of Modern India. New Delhi: Penguin Books India, 2006.xvi, 216.

Singh, Madhu. "Mahasweta Devi's Kunti and the Nishadin: a re-visionist text." Journal of the School of Language, Literature and Culture Studies 7 New Sereies (Spr 2007): 7- 15.

Singh, V.P. "The Crisi of the Girl- Child: a study of selected Indian Short-Stories in English Translation." Dialogue 2.1 (Jun 2006): 65- 72.

Sivasankari. Knit India Through Literature: Volume II –The East. Chennai : East West Books (Madras) Pvt. Ltd., 2000.xv,391.

Smitja, M. "Rising Out of the Ashes: the indomitable in Mahasweta Devi's Rudali and Mother 1084." Littcrit 33.2 – 64 (Dec 2007): 90- 97.

Srilata, K. "Green Mountains Outside the Kitchen Window: an ecocritical reading." Indian Journal of Ecocriticism 1. (Aug 2008): 55- 59.

Surya, Vasantha. "Unflinching Witness," Rev. of Rudali: From Fiction to Performance and Five Plays. Indian Review of Books 6.9 (16 Jun- 15 Jul 1997): 9-11.

Tellis, Ashley. "Old Testaments." Rev. of Old Women. Indian Review of Books 8.11 (Aug 16- Sep 15 1999): 32-33.

The denotified and Nomadic Tribes Rights action Group Newsletter, http://www.georgetown.edu/departments/pip/dnrag/budhan4.html

Tribal tours advertised on line. http://www.tsiindia.com/index.html

Tribal tour itinerary on line. Liza world Travel. http://www.lizaworldtravels.com/tribak-trail.html

Vanashree. "Witchcraft: Pain, Resistance and the Ceremony of Punishment- Mahasweta Devi's Bayen." Indian Journal of Gender Studies 17.2 (Jun 2010): 223-247.

Vijayalakshmi, M. "Reaching Out." Rev. of In a Forest, A Deer: stories. The Book Review 30.12 (Dec 2006): 9.

Vijayaraghavan, Sujatha. "Postcolonial Historiography a case study of Mahasweta Devi's The Queen of Jhansi." Journal of English Literature and Language 3.2 (Dec 2009): 13.

Vijayaraghavan, Sujatha. "Indian Women Writing / Righting the Nation in and through Fiction: a postcolonial perspective." Journal of The School of Language, Literature and Culture Studies 7 New Series (Spr 2007): 28-37.

Wenzel, Jennifer. "Epic Struggles over India's Forests in Mahasweta Devi's Short Fiction." Alif: Journal of Comparative Poetics 18 (1998): 127-158.

Yamuna. D.S. "Unveiling the Mundari World: a reading of Mahasweta Devi's Novel Chotti Munda and His Arrow." Littcrit 34.2-66 (Dec 2008): 103-110.

Author Bio

Dr. M. John Suganya is an expert in comparative studies, which has been her major research area. Her research studies focus on women studies. The research thesis on Mahaswetha Devi and Ambai has been an added value for the subaltern studies. She had her graduation, post-graduation and M.Phil. in English literature in various reputed institutions, respectively in MVM Government Arts College for Women, Dindigul, and Thiagarajar College of Arts and Science, Madurai. She had her Doctorate of Philosophy in PSG College of Arts & Science, Coimbatore, the most eminent institution which has produced great icons.

The author has been in teaching for more than eighteen years and has produced numerous research articles in reputed journals which have marked a huge milestone in her credentials. The intense research interest has produced more than one hundred and fifty research projects. To add a feather to the cap the writer has also authored a book entitled *Pygmalion as a Drama of Moral Virtues.*

She has also won the Best Teacher Award twice for her contributions in teaching and research. This work of art has a milieu of insight on the portrayal of women by the greatest playwrights known for their characterization and refraining to subject content. The experience in teaching for about two decades and skillful research knack has helped to bring valuable and credible content for the readers of selective studies.

Author Bio

Mr. Anith Prem Malaravan M is an expertise in language and literature. His research studies focus mainly on Women studies, Marginalization, along with English Language Teaching. The peripheral congeniality for concern in research towards women studies was through the comparative literature offered in his graduation. The writer had his graduation, post-graduation and Mater of Philosophy in English literature in various reputed institutions, respectively in The American College, Thiagarajar College of Arts and Science, Madurai and Madurai Kamaraj University.

The author has been in teaching for about two decades and has produced several research tutelages in reputed journals adding feather to his research credentials. The experience in teaching skillful research flair has rewarded in bringing this valuable and credible content for the readers of selective studies.